The Whole Part

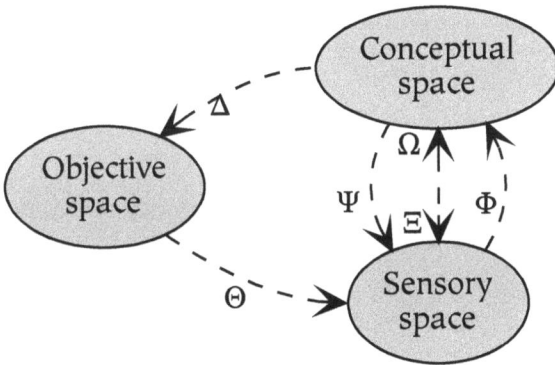

The Whole Part

http://theWholePart.com

ArborRhythms Publishing
Eugene, OR

Author: Alec M Rogers

ISBN: 978-0-9830376-4-4
Library of Congress Control Number: 2020904097

Revision History:

Revision 1.0	April 27th, 2020
Revision 1.1	September 1st, 2020

For all the angels I have loved,
and continue to love (wherever you are).

To the extent that I am able,
may I make the world a better place
for you and those you love.

Preface

The Whole Part describes a basic model of cognition that uses parts, wholes, and references to analyze both our material and mental experience.

The framework of continuous epistemological space, rather than discrete symbolic logic, is used to provide a formal foundation for thinking about reality. Mereological analysis of that space examines things in terms of their whole/part relationships, and referential analysis of that space examines things in terms of their reference/referent relationships. These analyses are used to illustrate the structure of our minds. Since our mental structures determine how reality is both sensed and conceptualized, understanding these structures clarifies which aspects of our experience are due to the world and which are due to various facets of our cognition.

People interested in how our minds work will particularly enjoy this book, since it provides a detailed analysis of the structure and operation of our cognition. This analysis relies on a basic model of cognition to provide an understanding of the relationship of wholes to parts, references to referents, and how those relationships influence and are influenced by cognition. This model is largely independent of various complexities in neuroscience and physics, although it is both motivated by those sciences and entirely compatible with them.

Finally, although everyone experiences both sensation and conceptualization, it is sometimes difficult to fully discriminate one from the other experientially. This ability is fairly critical; for example, to love the idea of something in place of the thing itself is a recipe for trouble. Therefore, the model developed in this book is intended to serve as a tool to both better understand and positively transform our lives.

Sincerely,
~alec

Table of Contents

Part 1

BACKGROUND

Without sensibility, no object would be given to us, and without understanding none would be thought. Thoughts without content are empty; intuitions without concepts are blind.

Immanuel Kant [Kant, 1781]

Chapter 1
Introduction

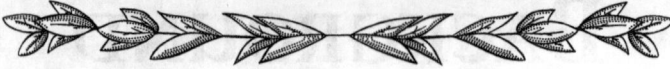

A book about wholes, parts, and references.

This book examines the world, both our experience of it and our thoughts about it, while focusing on the relations between wholes and parts. It examines our concepts, both how they are shaped by the world, and how they shape the world. These examinations use two analytic techniques: mereology (or analysis in terms of parts and wholes) and reference (or analysis in terms of references).

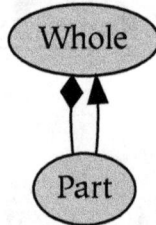

Figure 1.1: A whole and a part that is a reference to that whole.

To illustrate these mereological and referential relationships diagrammatically, various material and mental things are represented with ellipses and arrows. For example, Figure 1.1 shows that:

- Wholes are composed of parts (via diamond arrows).
- Parts may be references (via triangle arrows).
- Parts may referentially contain their wholes (in virtue of both arrows).

More detail about the notational and diagrammatic conventions used in this book, and UML diagrams in particular, is presented in appendix *Ideographic Conventions*, p. 214. The main content of this book is presented in four parts:

Part 1 introduces the book and provides a brief philosophical background of the main topics.

Part 2, entitled *Theory of Mereology and Reference,* is a short introduction to spaces and the dimensionality of spaces, particularly as they are structured by wholes, parts, and references. Wholes and parts form mereological spaces; wholes are formed by uniting parts, and parts are formed by dividing wholes. References and referents form referential spaces; references are formed by representing their referents, and referents are formed by being represented. Finally, there is a section introducing identity conditions for things within these different spaces and a section examining various edge cases.

Part 3, entitled *The Basic Model,* applies the theory of mereology and reference to human experience, thereby establishing the basic model of human cognition. Three spaces are constructed, which can be distinguished by their referential or epistemic level: physical space, subjective space, and conceptual space. Six relations between these spaces are also introduced: sensation, action, conceptualization, visualization, interpretation, and symbolization. In order to thoroughly understand these spaces, they are analyzed in terms of their parts and dimensionality.[1]

Part 4, entitled *Practical Implications,* is an informal look at various popular topics and paradoxes, cast within a mereological and referential framework. It explores questions such as: how does thought interfere with the perception of one's surroundings? What is the role of emotion with respect to concepts? Is consciousness a property of only one type of epistemic space, or

---

[1] Dimensionality is particularly well-suited to non-symbolic analysis since it is an aspect of continuous space, rather than any individuated entity within that space.

3

are there different types of consciousness associated with different spaces? Although no attempt is made to answer these questions definitively, the formal framework introduced in the earlier chapters provides a clear way to analyze them.

Chapter 2
History

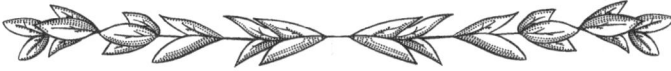

A brief history of the relation of wholes, parts, and references to the study of mind.

As this work presents a basic model of mind, its focus is <u>epistemological</u> rather than <u>ontological</u>. In practice, however, the determination of which facets of experience belong to mind as opposed to external reality is a matter of some debate. This chapter is a brief history of that debate, whose scope is the psychological and philosophical background within the Western and Indian traditions.

The science of wholes and parts (and to a lesser extent, references) in both traditions has a long history, going back as far as Plato in Greece (400 BCE) or the Vedas in India (3500 BCE). This science is closely related to the study of one and many, since the numeric relationship of a whole to its parts is one to many. Wholes, parts, and references are also related to the study of universals and particulars, and <u>absolute</u> and <u>relative</u> truths, although the precise relationship in these cases is more complex. The study of references in particular is relevant to understanding several important epistemic distinctions such as that between matter and mind, and between the intuitive and rational aspects of mind.

Reality

Some of the earliest discussions about wholes and parts derive from Indian philosophical debates about what is ultimately real (*paramarthasat*) and what is relatively real (*samvritisat*). These debates are continued in Western philosophy, where the reality of wholes and parts is often discussed in the context of *natural kinds*. The belief in natural kinds entails that the world is naturally (or more than just mentally) partitioned into various categories or types of *real* objects. Belief in natural kinds often leads to one of two general positions: one which asserts the reality of universals (or the abstract attributes of objects) and one which asserts the reality of particulars (or the concrete objects themselves). These two positions often result in two different criteria for what is real: one that pertains to material divisibility and one that pertains to the distinction between abstract and concrete entities.

Parts and Wholes

Numerous debates about material composition have occurred throughout history. In Indian philosophy, these arguments often begin by asking if the whole is the same as or different from its parts. This creates a dilemma if one assumes (either explicitly or implicitly) that only one thing can exist in a particular place at a particular time, in which case either the whole or the parts can be real (but not both).[2] In other words, wholes and parts are seen to be ontologically incompatible because they compete for *real* status at any given location.

The tension between parts and wholes has led some schools of philosophy to posit that parts are real and that wholes exist only in dependence on those parts.[3] These schools are called reductionistic because they *reduce* large-scale phenomena to small-scale phenomena, so that explanations of wholes are supplanted by explanations of parts. As a result, reductionists tend to believe that all things have an intrinsic nature that is defined in terms of their parts. All larger (composite) wholes exist only as nominal collections of those smaller atoms. This

---

[2] The implicit assumption that only one thing can exist in one place and time is possibly due to the structure of symbolic cognition. Although this assumption reduces redundancy, it also prevents overlap, which is unrealistic if objects in the world do in fact overlap.

[3] The belief that only atoms are ultimately real is shared by both Therevadan Buddhism and Greek atomistic philosophy.

philosophy is intuitively appealing because large things often visibly undergo more change than small things (as they can more easily be broken into parts). In other words, the smaller something is, the less likely it is to be visibly broken down, which makes it relatively permanent (and therefore more real). Reductionism therefore explains all phenomena as being founded on small or partless particles, or several types of <u>atoms</u>, which historically often included air, earth, fire, water, and sometimes space.

Despite the utility of reductionism, it is unduly one-sided as a theory of reality. For example, why would one believe that smaller parts are always a better basis for causal explanation than larger wholes? Similarly, why would one believe that the small is the *cause* of the large, when causation requires a temporal separation between a cause and its effects that is not present between parts and their whole?

To remedy the reductionistic bias, <u>holistic</u> philosophies emphasize the opposite point of view: the fundamental reality of the larger whole. Historically, the emphasis on whole-based (or holistic) as opposed to part-based (or reductionistic) explanations of reality often coincides with the schism between the spiritual and secular aspects of life. More precisely, spiritual and selfless traditions tend to gravitate toward whole-based explanations of reality, while materialistic and selfish traditions tend to gravitate toward part-based explanations. Perhaps this tendency is not surprising given that what is divine is most often considered as a whole, and one's self is most often considered as a part.[4]

Numerous non-monotheistic traditions are also holistic. For example, polytheistic Brahmanical traditions extol the universal soul (*Brahman*) as opposed to the individual soul (*paramatman*), and non-theistic Buddhist traditions often emphasize *dependent co-origination*, or the mutual dependence of all parts

---

[4] In fact, God is often considered to be *the ultimate whole*, a belief that forms the basis of both pantheism and panentheism. Similarly, consistently regarding one's self as a whole as opposed to a part is the basis of egotism.

(*pratityasamutpada*). In modern Western philosophy, a number of explicitly holistic arguments were made by Hegel, who argued that parts become more complete in the context of their wholes.

The perceived incompatibility of wholes and parts has also led philosophers to adopt various forms of nominalism. For example, the Indian philosopher Chandrakirti (ca. 650 CE), after thoroughly analyzing the ways in which a whole may relate to its parts, concludes that wholes are neither the same nor different from their parts.[5] Since a given object is not essentially either a whole or a part, he further concludes that objects exist only in a relative or nominal sense.[6]

Particulars and Universals

An important distinction between two types of mental content is characterized by various Western philosophers in terms of the requirement to experience an external world. Knowledge about mind and various mental activities does not require such experience, so it is called *a priori* experience: such knowledge is "prior to" experience. Knowledge about the nature of matter does require experience of the world, so it is called *a posteriori*: such knowledge is gained only "after the fact" of experience. Typically, *a priori* experience is characterized by generic <u>universals</u>, and *a posteriori* experience is characterized by specific <u>particulars</u>.

Not all philosophies regard universals as mental and particulars as physical. Platonism, one of the earliest holistic

---

[5] Chandrakirti frequently talks about a whole and its parts as they relate to a person, in which context they are referred to as a "self" and its "aggregates", respectively.

[6] There are several arguments in Indian philosophy that a whole is neither the same as its parts nor different from them. For example, a whole is not the same as its parts because a thing cannot be both one and many at the same time. Another argument is that if various parts of a whole are missing, the whole continues to exist, therefore none of the particular parts are essential. On the other hand, a whole cannot be other than its parts, since removing all the parts will also remove the whole. For more detail, see the section on sevenfold reasoning in [Thakchoe, 2011] or similar arguments in [Wasserman, 2018].

philosophies in the Western philosophical tradition, holds that universal properties are real and particular objects are not.[7] For example, unchanging universals such as *horseness* and *brownness* intersect to form ephemeral particulars such as brown horses. Similarly, the universal of horseness can be regarded as an abstract union of the properties shared by many particular horses.

Holistic theories such as Platonism, which treat wholes as more important than parts, also tend to prioritize mental and immaterial entities over physical and material entities. This may be a result of the more obvious impermanence of large particulars (i.e., being real is commonly associated with permanence, and large particulars tend to be ephemeral). Similarly, immaterial objects such as thoughts are sometimes regarded as permanent because immaterial properties are not visible, and therefore are not subject to visible change.

Table 1.2a: Universals and particulars with respect to the distinctions between whole/part and mind/matter.

	Whole	Part
Mind	Universals	
Matter		Particulars

As a result of these considerations, particulars are often seen as small (material) parts, while universals are often seen as larger (immaterial) wholes. This conjunction is expressed in Table 1.2a, which should be understood as illustrating a common historical occurrence rather than a logical necessity. The table expresses a tension because wholes and parts are regarded as having the

---

[7] Platonism is a denial of materialism because it posits that material things are actually a bundle of ideal forms. Platonism (or Platonic Realism) and Materialism are both construed in this context as types of realism: one accepts the reality of universals and the other accepts the reality of particulars. In this work, universals are treated as valid *mental* phenomena, regardless of their ontological status.

same material or immaterial substance, while universals and particulars are not. In other words, since wholes are composed of parts, both wholes and parts are seen as material if one is a materialist, or as immaterial if one is an idealist. Almost always, however, universals are regarded as abstract and particulars are regarded as concrete. The view presented in this book is that all sensations are unique; therefore, conceptual wholes composed of those parts are also particulars. However, conceptual wholes can become *abstract* when they are created top-down from symbolic references, and it is that abstractness which is characterized as immaterial.[8]

Mind and Matter

The relation between mind and matter is a primary concern for any model of cognition, since a model that describes how cognition works is bound to be problematic without some notion of what cognition is. In this work, wholes and parts are used to specify the location of references and their referents, while the relation between mind and matter relies on references.

The study of reference exists in a wide number of disciplines. Words are probably the most well-known form of references, so the study of references is essential to linguistics. References are also essential to thoughts, and they are therefore essential to psychology. In the context of this book, references are used to define *mind*. Mind is that which refers to something, in addition to whatever else it may be. In more philosophical language, mind has <u>intentionality</u>, while matter does not.

Of course, the discriminability of mind and matter does not entail that they are entirely different kinds of things. For example,

---

[8] The relationship between abstraction and materiality is explored further in subsequent chapters. Briefly, abstraction entails that things lose some of their characteristic (particular) properties, such as their specific location within space or time. For example, an abstraction based on two green things may have no properties associated with place or time if the green things are not collocated, but it has the property of color since greenness belongs to both.

the philosophy called *neutral monism* maintains that there is only one kind of stuff, which exists prior to being differentiated into mind and matter. This view was described by William James, who said that mind and matter are both "pure experience", and that the duality of knower and known is a derivative notion. In his view, knowing (or <u>awareness</u>) is not a thing; rather, it is a relation between two parts of experience (i.e., between mental references and their physical referents).

Neutral monism can be expressed in more physical terms by substituting James' singular mental event (or experience) with Baruch Spinoza's singular physical thing (or "the one substance"). In the latter case, because *substance* takes on attributes of body and mind, even objects such as rocks have some form of mind (a doctrine known as <u>panpsychism</u>). Although panpsychism requires a very liberal interpretation of mind, it is not problematic if one regards the various features of rocks such as their layers and chips as references to (or even as memories of) things that happened to those rocks over the course of their existence. This poetic interpretation, of course, does not entail that rocks are smart in the same way as are animals.[9] In particular, although matter may be conscious at some non-referential level, this reflexive or intransitive <u>consciousness</u> is different from the intentional mental <u>awareness</u> that requires some degree of reference.[10]

The main point of this discussion is that objects belonging to different categories of things may also be seen as belonging to the same, more general category. By recasting objects in this way, it

---

[9] Although as Steven Pinker said, "Rocks are smarter than cats, because rocks have the good sense to go away when you kick them." (see [Pinker, 2007]).

[10] In this book, "consciousness" is reflexive or intransitive, while "awareness" is always intentional. In other words, consciousness is direct or pre-reflective, while awareness is necessarily reflective (i.e., it is awareness *of something else*). Therefore, while arbitrary matter may have some form of consciousness, only a mind can have awareness. In Indian philosophy, reflexive consciousness is known as *svasamvedana*, where it is likened to a lamp that illuminates itself (see [Kellner, 2011]).

11

is possible to reinterpret dualistic theories as monistic theories. For nominalistic theories, this reinterpretation is particularly simple, since things are not inherently categorized as wholes/ parts or referents/references, just as arbitrary objects are neither small nor big except in relation to other objects.[11] However, if one avoids characterizing reality with any analysis or categorization whatsoever, then it becomes impossible to express the nature of its one constitutive type.

Sensation, Concepts, and Symbols

The distinctions between the sensory, conceptual, and symbolic aspects of mind are essential to models of cognition. These distinctions are known by many names and run parallel to many other well-known dichotomies. In Indian philosophy, for example, subjective (symbolic) truths are known as relative truths and objective truths are known as absolute or ultimate truths.[12] In terms of Dual Process Theory, sensation and concepts correspond to System 1 and symbols correspond to System 2.[13] Several of these distinctions are shown in Table 1.2b. As the granularity of the first column of this table suggests, an essential role of a basic model of cognition is to clarify various aspects of our experience by providing a more precise categorical scheme. According to multiple philosophical traditions, this effort is especially difficult for categories corresponding to nonconceptual content because dividing things into wholes and parts, one and many, references and referents, or even mind and matter, are all

---

[11] This point of view does not imply that "everything is relative". For example, although a rock may be called soft, it does not make a decent pillow.

[12] Discerning the relative and the absolute in the Indian philosophical context is of great importance, since doing so is a precursor to correctly understanding and operating in the world.

[13] This correspondence is revised slightly in subsequent chapters, when concrete concepts are distinguished from abstract concepts.

inherently conceptual (or relative) categorizations.[14] Therefore, to study nonconceptual experience from a conceptual point of view is often regarded as a bit problematic, if not outright paradoxical. However, by analyzing the symbolic/subsymbolic dichotomy from the symbolic point of view, it may at least be possible to conceptually understand the subsymbolic aspects of experience (i.e., by extricating them from the symbolic aspects).

Table 1.2b: The symbolic, conceptual, sensory, and objective distinctions as they most closely align with several other dichotomies.

Symbolic	**Relative**	***A priori***	**Top-down**	**System 2**	**Universal, Abstract**
Conceptual					
Sensory		***A posteriori***	**Bottom-up**	**System 1**	**Particular, Concrete**
Objective	**Absolute**				

One difficulty with Table 1.2b is that it oversimplifies several of its constituent distinctions. In particular, the distinction between absolute/relative is sometimes understood as two omnipresent aspects of reality, while this table depicts them as endpoints of a single continuum. Similarly, bottom-up and top-down are better understood as directions instead of absolute locations, so placing them within the context of this table conflates direction with location. That said, this table does approximate the alignment of several relevant distinctions across a wide range of literature as well as raise questions about the relation of these categories to one another that are pertinent to subsequent chapters.

As the categories presented in Table 1.2b are extremely generic, it may add clarity to examine how those categories relate

---

[14] For example, the Kantian tradition defines several categories of things that are inherently *a priori,* such as number. Similarly, the Buddhist tradition defines any verbal expression as relative (or imputed) truth.

to a particular example. Our own *self* is an important and commonly cited example, which will be explored throughout this work. The study of the self has a long history; for example, the Nyaya school of Indian philosophy claims that the self (or *atman*) exists within the world as an eternal, singular thing. Later Indian and Buddhist philosophy took exception to this view, arguing that neither a personal self nor anything else in the world could be either permanent or singular, and categorized the self as relative (*samvritisat*) rather than absolute (*paramarthasat*). Immanuel Kant made similar claims, enumerating several *a priori* categories such as quantity (including notions of both singularity and plurality) that can be known independently of the world, thereby ensuring their status as universals and further providing a cognitive foundation for mathematics. The basic model of cognition developed in this work continues these traditions, distinguishing sensory from conceptual aspects of mind, and discussing how these aspects of mind relate to the objective world.[15]

Cognitive Science

Modern cognitive science takes a philosophical stance regarding the relation between subjective and objective (or mind and matter) known as <u>indirect realism</u>. According to this theory, everything outside the body is represented inside the body, both symbolically and subsymbolically. This view exists within a context of numerous other possibilities:

---

[15] Even if the world cannot be expressed directly, it is possible to make conditional statements about it.

0. **Nondualism**: There are no basic types of things that can be categorized with absolute accuracy.

1. **Monism**: Mental and physical entities are the result of an analysis which is not ontologically valid.

   1.1 Materialism: Mind (or consciousness) is ill-defined and not a singular phenomenon or even a coherent notion (see [Dennett, 1991]).

   1.2 Idealism: Matter does not exist except as mental stuff.

   1.3 Neutral Monism: There is only one kind of stuff, which is a combination of mind and matter.

2. **Dualism**: Mind and matter are different principles or kinds of things. In Cartesian dualism they occupy different locations, while in Samkhya philosophy they exist on different ontological levels (i.e., as prakriti and purusha).

   2.1 Direct Realism: The philosophy that perception engages directly with external objects.

   2.2 Indirect Realism: The philosophy that perception engages with external objects only indirectly, as mediated by references.

3. **Pluralism**: There are many basic types of substances.

Since the predominant view is that subjective universes are constituted by references to the larger, physical universe, the basic model developed in this book follows suit.[16] However, all of these philosophical points of view present some true aspect of reality.

---

[16] The less common view is that the physical universe consists of references to subjective universes. Although this book tries not to take sides about the ultimate ground of reality, it necessarily adopts a point of view for the purposes of presentation.

Summary

Although the topics in this chapter serve as important philosophical background, most of the book deals with more practical issues within cognitive science. Therefore, the next two sections of this book are less concerned with the question of "what is mind?" and more concerned with "how does mind work?". The final section of this book returns to these topics in order to investigate mind and world, the concept of self in relation to our experience, and the discrimination of various aspects of relative and absolute experience.

Part 2

THEORY OF MEREOLOGY AND REFERENCE

What is it [...] that divides the atmosphere from the water? It is necessary that there should be a common boundary which is neither air nor water but is without substance, because a body interposed between two bodies prevents their contact, and this does not happen in water with air. [...] Therefore a surface is the common boundary of two bodies which are not continuous, and does not form part of either one or the other, for if the surface formed part of it, it would have divisible bulk, whereas, however, it is not divisible and nothingness divides these bodies the one from the other.

Leonardo da Vinci [Varzi, 2015].

This book uses two types of analyses: <u>mereological</u> and <u>referential</u>. Mereological spaces are structured by the whole/part relationship, and referential spaces are structured by the reference/referent relationship. Mereological and referential analyses of a given space are <u>nominalistic</u> analyses that create individual *things* within that space.[17] They are nominal in the sense that the structure of space is determined by the operation that is used to name or categorize it. As a result of these analyses, things can be divided into four general types: <u>wholes</u>, <u>parts</u>, <u>references</u>, and <u>referents</u>. However, most things may be any or all of these four types of things, depending on one's point of view. For example, a word written on a piece of paper is a whole of many cellulose fibers, a part of a book, a reference to a concept, and the referent of this sentence.

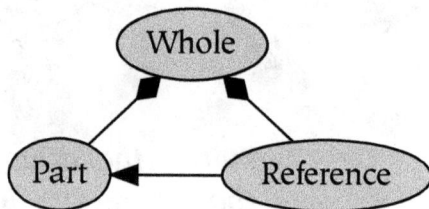

Figure 2: A whole, a part, and a part that is a reference.

As an example, Figure 2 shows the way that references play a role in both mereological and referential spaces at the same time. To make this example more concrete, suppose that the diagram describes a *room*, a *vase*, and a piece of *paper* that has the word "vase" written on it (objects that are *a whole, a part*, and *a reference*, respectively). Both the vase and the paper are parts of the room, at least temporarily. The word on the paper ("vase") is a reference to the vase object. Therefore, the word on the paper is both a thing in-and-of-itself and a reference to something else, as indicated in the diagram by the two attached arrows. In other words, it has a dual role: it has a mereological role (in relation to the paper, the ink, etc.) and a referential role (in relation to the

---

[17] The use of the term "things" is deliberately generic; this term is delineated further in section *Epistemic Universes* (p. 60)

vase object).[18] Even the vase itself has a dual role, since it is both a part and a referent.

The multiple roles of the objects in this example create two different kinds of space: referential space (which is structured by references) and physical or mereological space (which is structured by wholes and parts). As the former space requires subjective interpretation, it may also be characterized as mental space. These differing types of spaces illustrate that the concept of space is used very generally in the context of this book as a metaphor to describe both physical and mental reality. Space should also be understood generally in that it is high-dimensional or open-dimensional. Understanding space in this way is particularly important because a central thesis of this work is that the dimensionality of space is shared with all things within that space. As a consequence, if the physical universe is four-dimensional, then our world contains four-dimensional objects as parts, and cannot contain three-dimensional objects except as abstractions.[19]

As far as possible, space is left unanalyzed. Although analysis of physical space may determine things to be one, many, wholes, parts, references, or referents, space itself does not have a predetermined structure or fixed number of dimensions. In other words, physical space and the material within it are not inherently *many things* or *one thing*, so applying these mutually exclusive concepts to physical space would limit comprehension. This stance avoids conjectures about reality that are impossible to determine, and leaves open the possibility that space is inexpressible *as it is experienced*.

---

[18] According to an Indian metaphor called the *Net of Indra*, the universe is like a net of jewels, each of which reflects all the others. This suggests that all objects are both references and referents. Shantideva (ca. 8th century CE) similarly characterizes all objects as having a relative nature and an absolute nature.

[19] It may clarify things to think in terms of "events" and "spacetime" instead of in terms of "things" and "space", since the former terms connote more than three dimensions.

Chapter 3
Mereological Space

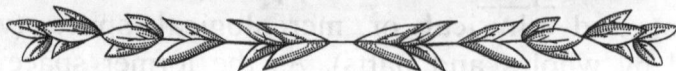

A mereological space is structured with wholes and parts.

Mereological spaces are structured by the whole/part relationship. Both physical spaces and sensory spaces can be structured mereologically; for example, a tree is a part of a forest and the sensation of a tree is a part of the sensation of a forest. However, the relation between a referent and its reference is not mereological. In other words, symbols are not necessarily either parts or wholes of what they symbolize.

All parts of a mereological whole share the dimensionality of that whole. For example, there are no 2-D surfaces in a 3-D world, and there are no 3-D objects in a 4-D world; therefore, it is not correct to conceive of a 2-D line existing in a 3-D space from a mereological point of view (although it may be a useful approximation or an interesting epistemological limit). This means that abstract elements such as points, lines, and planes are incapable of constituting physical space. In other words, parts have a spatial extent along every dimension of the space that contains them, just as a piece of paper has more than two dimensions.

Further, for any two entities A and B in a mereological space, one of the following relations holds:[20]

1. Neither is a part of the other (i.e., the entities are disjoint).
2. A is a part of B (i.e., B is *a whole* of A).

---

[20] These relations are stated using the improper part operator (≤) instead of the proper part operator (<). If proper parts are used as the basis for our meronomy, then case (4) and case (1) are indistinguishable.

3. B is a part of A (i.e., A is *a whole* of B).
4. Both are parts of each other (i.e., the things are identical).
5. There is no definite parthood relationship between the entities (i.e., A is neither a part of B, nor is A not a part of B).

These relations are illustrated graphically in Figure 2.3a. The fifth case is somewhat problematic, because there is no simple answer to the question "Is A a part of B?". To state that either "A is a part of B" or "A is not a part of B" would be incorrect: one part of A *is* a part of B and another part of A *is not* a part of B. It is tempting to say that "A is a part of B" AND "A is not a part of B", but expressing that is beyond the capacity of ordinary (bivalent) logic.

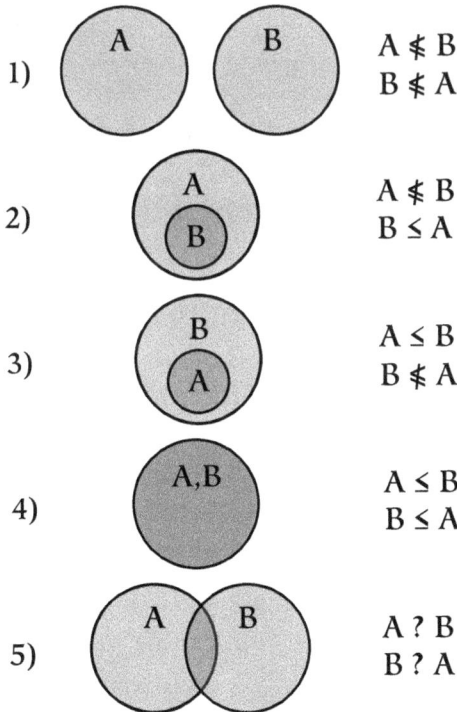

Figure 2.3a: The five possible mereological relations.

6)
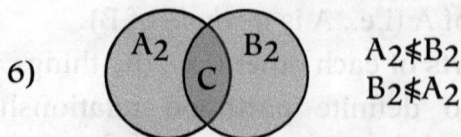

$A_2 \nleq B_2$
$B_2 \nleq A_2$

**Figure 2.3b: Recategorizing overlap
as three non-overlapping parts.**

In order to ensure that the part operation imposes at least a partial order on a given space, overlap must be prevented by categorizing any overlapping space as a new entity, as in Figure 2.3b.[21] Epistemologically, however, it may make more sense to extend logic so that it accurately describes uncertainty, rather than removing all overlap (which may be impossible in some cases).[22] To illustrate this, a continuous version of logic is introduced in appendix *Formal Summary* (p. 177).

2.3.1 Wholes

Wholes are composed of their parts.

Figure 2.3.1 shows a whole that is composed of two parts. Although reading this figure from the top down indicates a whole being made of two parts, the orientation of the figure makes no functional difference since all structural relationships are indicated by the directionality of the arrows. Therefore, from a procedural point of view, a branch like the one depicted can be understood as either a division or a collection. As a division, it

---

[21] A *partial order* is one which has equivalence classes (e.g., classes of objects for which neither of those objects is a part of the other). A space is *totally ordered* if all objects in that space are either parts or wholes of all other objects in that space.

[22] It also makes sense practically if there is a cognitive dis-ease with overlapping parts when overlap is not accommodated in one way or another (i.e., if our choice of logic affects our tolerance of ambiguous situations in the world).

creates parts out of a larger whole, and as a collection, it creates a whole out of smaller parts.

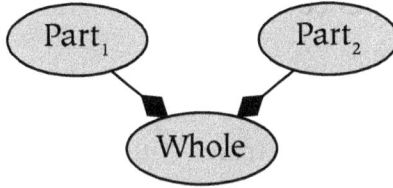

Figure 2.3.1: A whole in relation to two parts.

Because there is no mereological relation depicted between Part$_1$ and Part$_2$, one might assume that they do not overlap. In symbolic logic, however, this may only indicate that overlap cannot be expressed between discrete entities using the part/whole relation. Unfortunately, this inability to easily express overlap is problematic given the abundance of overlap in the world. For example, arbitrary parts of a tree such as the bark are partially coextensive with the trunk, so neither is entirely a part of the other.

As a result, any overlap which is not analytically removed is most often represented in separate hierarchies (i.e., mereological space within a single hierarchy most often has non-overlapping parts). Further, it is common for the parts within a single hierarchy to form a partition of that whole. Parts form a partition of their respective whole if the parts do not overlap and the space of that whole is completely covered by those parts. For example, *apples* and *oranges* do not form a partition of *fruits*, because there are some fruits that are neither apples nor oranges.[23]

---

[23] Partitions can be easily formed by recursively creating dichotomies of a whole, since a part and its complement always create a partition.

2.3.2 Parts

Parts compose their wholes.

Figure 2.3.2 depicts exactly the same information as the figure in the previous section: a whole that is composed of two parts. In both cases, the figure illustrates that the same object can be nominally constituted by either one whole or two parts.[24] Similarly, because the boundary is nominal, the presence or absence of a <u>boundary</u> does not materially affect the composition of the whole. In other words, although the universe may be mentally divided into things, the dividing lines do not have any concrete existence.[25] This finding is non-trivial, since it implies that the boundary that does the dividing does not occupy the same space as the things it divides. For example, when points divide lines, 0-D things partition a 1-D space. The same principle applies when lines divide planes; in both cases, the extent of the partitioning element is zero along the dimension of the space that it divides. [26]

Although this may not sound significant, it is an important departure from point-set topology, which is the field of mathematics that is typically used to describe space. Point-set topology assumes the existence of partless parts (or points) that constitute spaces of higher dimensionality. For example, a three-dimensional space is made up of an uncountable infinity of zero-dimensional parts. While this analysis works mathematically, it

---

[24] The number of things in a mereological space is therefore a function of one's point of view. For example, whether a jungle is considered to be one forest or one thousand trees does not change the reality of the situation, since in both cases the jungle has the same spatiotemporal extent or shape.
[25] However, there is usually some basis in the world in virtue of which the mental division is made. In more technical language, *fiat* (or nominal) boundaries often correspond to *bona fide* (or actual) boundaries.
[26] If this were not the case, the partitioning elements themselves would be parts, which has side effects such as preventing objects from making contact with each other.

is problematic from a psychological point of view (for further details, see appendix *Formal Summary*, p. 177).

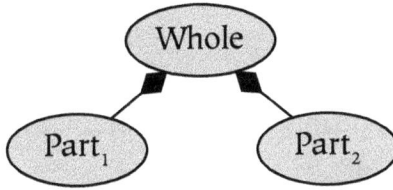

Figure 2.3.2: Two parts in relation to a whole.

These several principles of point-free-topology may be informally summarized as follows:

♦ The dimensionality of a part is always equal to the dimensionality of its whole.

♦ Boundaries such as dividing lines are nominal (i.e., they are not parts of the things that they divide).

♦ Space is not a whole of partless particles and is not a part of a whole-less whole (i.e., it is not bounded below or above).

2.3.3 Mereological Identity

*Mereological identity entails both
internal identity and external identity.*

Two things are mereologically identical if they have both the same wholes and parts.

If two objects have the same parts, they are <u>internally identical</u>. For example, the internal or material identity of a car may entail that it has four wheels, two axles, a body, a steering wheel, and an engine as parts. Internal identity is closely associated with essentialism, since the essence of a thing is generally considered to be internal to that thing.[27]

---

[27] For reasons discussed later, human minds seem particularly prone to the essentialist view. However, the argument against essentialism that no thing

If two objects have the same wholes, they are <u>externally</u> <u>identical</u>. External identity is often stated in terms of functional properties. For example:

A thing is a chair if you can sit on it.

However, all definitions using properties can also be stated using the language of wholes and parts. For example, the previous sentence can be restated as:[28]

A thing is a chair if it is a part of the class of all things on which you can sit.

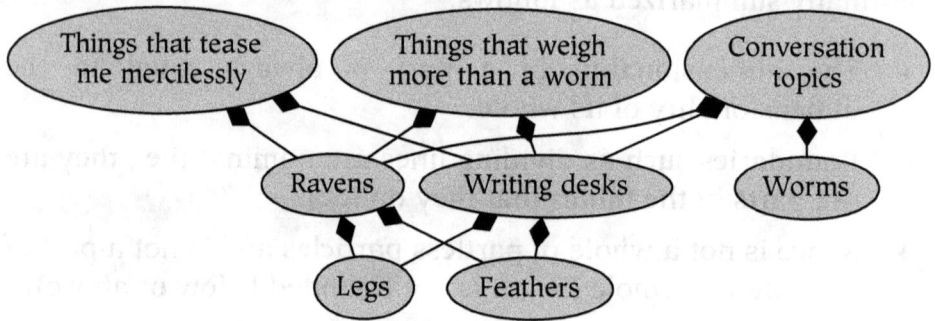

Figure 2.3.3: The mereological identity of ravens and writing desks.

In order to illustrate the role of mereological context, Figure 2.3.3 depicts several of the wholes and parts of ravens, writing desks, and worms. In that mereological context, ravens, writing desks, and worms are parts of larger wholes, while ravens and writing desks are also wholes of smaller parts (worms are atoms because they have no parts).[29] Because ravens and writing desks have the *same* wholes and parts in this limited context, they are both externally and internally identical, and therefore

---

is entirely independent of its context is made by numerous movements in psychology and philosophy.

[28] Mathematically, this corresponds to the <u>extensional</u> definition of a superset, rather than the <u>intensional</u> definition of the set using a property.

[29] Writing desks have feathers in virtue of their quill pens.

26

mereologically identical. In mathematical terminology, there is an isomorphism between ravens and writing desks.

2.3.4 Mereological Edge Cases

There are two mereological edge cases:
wholeless wholes and partless parts.

The edge cases of the whole/part continuum are whole-less wholes and part-less parts, or ultimate wholes and ultimate parts. Ultimate objects are particularly interesting because things with no wholes lack external properties, and things with no parts lack internal properties. This makes them paradoxical to talk about or even think about, although they figure into our mental lives frequently.

In mathematical mereology, a space with upper or lower limits on the operation of parthood is called *bounded above* or *bounded below*, respectively. If there are no such bounds, that space is called open (i.e., open above or open below).

2.3.4.1 Ultimate Wholes

A mereological thing that has no wholes is
an ultimate whole, or a universe.

The ultimate whole is the biggest thing. Only one ultimate whole can exist within a single mereological space, since if two ultimate wholes exist in the same space, then there would be a larger (conceptual) whole that consists of both.[30] In an epistemological context, the ultimate whole is similar to the mathematical notion of the set of all sets. In an ontological context, the ultimate whole is known as *the universe*.

---

[30] This corresponds to a thesis in mathematics known as *unrestricted composition*.

The term "universe" derives from the Latin *universum*, meaning "[every object] combined into one". Unfortunately, this term may also designate an object that is not the largest thing (i.e., if one believes in things that extend beyond the universe, such as multiverses). In this work, the word "universe" is used as originally intended; the universe is that thing which is a whole of everything else. As with space, the universe is open-dimensional. Therefore, although the universe is typically described with spatial (i.e., atemporal) metaphors, it is better understood as a long-lasting event because it has both spatial and temporal extents.

$$\boxed{\text{Universe}}$$

Figure 2.3.4a: Universes are wholeless wholes.

Because there is nothing to which the universe can be compared other than itself or parts of itself, it is difficult to define. One could call it large in relation to its parts, but that would entail that all things are large things. As the universe cannot have external properties, it cannot be big or small, heavy or light. In other words, since definitions are always given in terms of other things (i.e., they are relative), it is not possible to define "the one without a second".[31] For example, to call the universe a unity implies that there is some plurality with which it can be contrasted, which is not the case. However, while it may be mistaken to make a relative statement about the universe, it may help to counter prior misconceptions. For example, the assertion that the universe is one entity might be correct in so far as it counters the assertion that the universe is a multiplicity of independent things.

Conceptually, the universe is a space without limits; it is not finite or closed, which is required by wholes that have no further

---

[31] "One without a second" (*ekam evadvitiyam*) is a euphemism for Brahman, the ultimate reality underlying all phenomena, mentioned in Chandogya Upanishad (chapter 6 section 2).

wholes.[32] Closed space is paradoxical, since one could imagine going to the end of the universe and then moving a bit beyond that location. If that is possible, then the universe is not closed. If that is not possible, it suggests that the obstruction is a thing that lies beyond the boundary, which also entails that the world is not closed. In other words, if boundaries exist only as the division between parts, then wholes which are not parts in any larger whole do not have boundaries. On that account, universes *cannot* have a boundary because there is nothing for them to be divided from, and therefore they are unbounded by definition.[33]

2.3.4.2 Ultimate Parts
A mereological thing that has no parts
is an ultimate part, or an atom.

An ultimate part is the smallest thing, and is called an atom. The term "atom" derives from the Greek *atomos*, which means uncuttable or indivisible.[34] For space to be atomic, or to have parts which are atoms, means that the process of creating parts cannot occur indefinitely. In other words, they are things that cannot be subdivided.

Figure 2.3.4b: Atoms are partless parts.

---

[32] Space could also be non-Euclidean, such as a toroidal space that wraps around like a donut.

[33] This discussion of spatial boundaries also applies to temporal boundaries, a topic addressed in section *The Physical Universe* (p. 62).

[34] The name "atom" stuck to the particle it was originally used to describe, even though that particle ceased to be regarded as indivisible due to the discovery of sub-atomic particles. The quest to find increasingly small particles has continued, and today it remains an open question whether or not matter has such smallest units.

Atoms have no parts in virtue of which they can be distinguished from one another. Therefore, all atoms are internally identical, and can only be distinguished from one another in virtue of their larger wholes. As a result, the atom represents the limit of reductionism as an explanatory strategy; it is not possible for reductionism to explain what an atom is in terms of its parts, *because it has no parts*.[35]

Although both atoms and points are partless and therefore indivisible, atoms are not equivalent to points in the mathematical sense. Atoms have a spatial extent, whereas points have no extent; therefore, atoms exist in discrete space, while points exist in continuous space. More information about the difference between points and atoms is presented in appendix *Formal Summary* (p. 177).

---

[35] In modern physics, particles are defined by appealing to various properties such as *handedness* and *spin*. However, since these particles cannot be distinguished in virtue of their parts, it becomes a considerable problem to explain why different properties are associated with different particles (since in absence of parts, these particles have no internal differences).

Chapter 4
Referential Space

A referential space is structured with references and referents.

Referential spaces are structured by the reference/referent relationship. The things that are named are called referents, and the things that name them are called references. References are directional, in that references point to their referents.

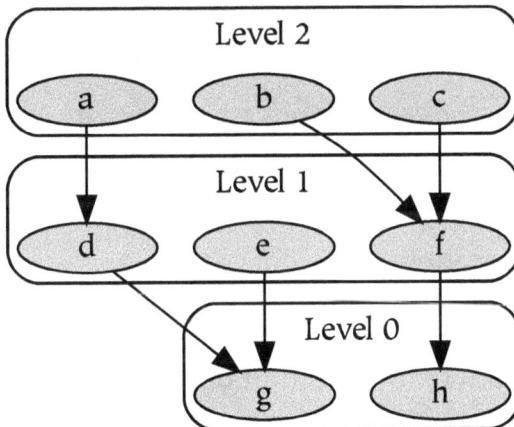

Figure 2.4: References stratify things according to their referential level.

References are not mereological because the relationship between a reference and its referent has nothing to do with whether they are parts of one another, although references and the referents on which they depend often form parts of a mereological space. References are discrete, although the referential relation may in general be continuous (in which case it is called <u>reflection</u>).

Referential space itself is typically divided into subspaces of referenced objects and referencing objects. Because references can in turn be referents, a stratification of <u>referential level</u> is established. As Figure 2.4 illustrates, references form referential chains (depicted vertically) that may pass through multiple referential levels (depicted horizontally), mapping onto referents in lower levels. Things on the bottom level of the diagram have a referential level of zero and are not references to anything else (they are "things in themselves"). The referential level of each successive level is one more than the level to which it refers. Therefore, referential level indicates the distance of a reference from ground, or its ultimate object of reference.

2.4.1 References

References refer to referents.

The word reference derives from the Latin *referent*, which means "bringing back". References are things that are capable of referencing or denoting a referent, so the <u>existence</u> of a reference implies that its referent can be found in the world. There may be multiple references for a single referent, but a reference can only refer to a single referent, a relation depicted in Figure 2.4.1.

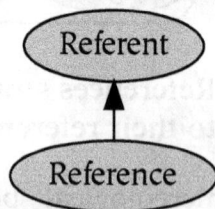

Figure 2.4.1: A reference in relation to its referent.

References are both things themselves as well as things that refer to other things. They do not need to resemble their referents in any way, a principle known in linguistics as the *arbitrariness of signs.* Therefore, the significance of references *as* references does not derive from what they are, but from what they represent or signify.[36] They play a crucial role in cognitive psychology, where the referenced objects of the external world become referential parts of the space of subjective awareness.

2.4.2 Referents

Referents are denoted by references.

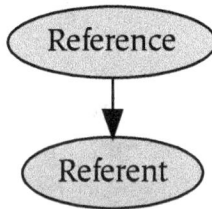

Figure 2.4.2: A referent in relation to its reference.

Referents are the things which references point to, reference, denote, or name. Referents may be denoted by multiple references, and they may in turn be references to other referents, but they do not have a mereological structure. Thus, although referents may have dimensionality in virtue of being parts of mereological spaces, their only structure within referential space is derived from their referential relationships. In other words, references and referents are atoms within discrete referential spaces, and consequently, there is no such thing as a half of a reference.

---

[36] Although references *can* be understood in terms of what they are (i.e., in and of themselves), they are referentially significant because they represent something else.

2.4.3 Referential Identity

Referential identity entails that two references refer to the same referent.

The notion of identity can be applied to references in at least two ways. Referential identity means that two things are identical if they have the same referent. For example, the references "the first man to walk on the moon" and "Neil Armstrong" have the same referent, so these two statements are referentially identical. References also establish an identity between a reference and its referent.

Since references can represent something unlike themselves, the validity of the reference/referent mapping is established via isomorphism. For example, isomorphism between a reference and its referent, such as the concept river$_\varphi$ and a physical river, entails that the concept relates to other concepts just as the river relates to other physical objects. This relational basis for identity allows a reference to be independent of its referent; for example, the concept of the river may be contextually similar to the physical river without needing to have identical physical characteristics, such as being physically wet.

2.4.4 Referential Edge Cases

There are several referential edge cases: ultimate referents, ultimate references, self-referential references, empty references, and full references.

There are two primary edge cases in referential spaces: ultimate references and ultimate referents. Ultimate references cannot be referenced, and ultimate referents are non-referential. Unlike parts, which require a relation between exactly two objects, references have two additional edge cases that involve only one object: references that refer to themselves (or self-references) and references that refer to nothing (or empty references). This section also introduces full references, which are the <u>complement</u> of empty references.

2.4.4.1 Ultimate Referents
An ultimate referent does not reference any other referent.

Figure 2.4.4a: An ultimate referent is not a reference to any other referent.

In some philosophical theories such as Kant's, ultimate referents are things-in-themselves (*dinge an sich*) that form a referential ground of being; without them, references become vacuous. In other words, ultimate referents are particularly significant because they create a grounding that gives all other references meaning. If this grounding is not present, then all references become meaningless. However, what are ultimate referents from one point of view may not be ultimate referents from another, so while it may be necessary to begin with a referential ground, that referential ground is not necessarily unique.

A profound example of references with no ultimate referents is a dictionary, since all of the words in a dictionary are defined by other words. Therefore, their definitions consist of references that are eventually circular. For example, if an alien who didn't know *any* words tried to find the definition of a word in a dictionary, the definition of that word would necessarily contain other words that the alien does not know, which would entail looking up further words. This situation involves an infinite regress; if the alien does not know the meaning of any words to begin with, how is it possible to learn even one of them? The only way to break this endless cycle is to know the meaning (experientially) of one or more of the words, and in this process, those words become ultimate referents.[37]

2.4.4.2 Ultimate References
Ultimate references cannot be referenced.

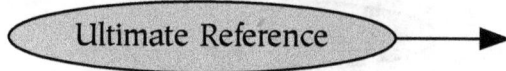

Figure 2.4.4b: An ultimate reference is not a referent of any other reference.

NB: It is not possible to talk about ultimate references, because to do so would be to refer to them.

2.4.4.3 Self-Referential References
Self-Referential references refer to themselves.

Self-referential references *seem* possible, unlike the obviously impossible example of a (proper) part that contains its whole. However, <u>self-reference</u> is problematic and the basis for innumerable paradoxes.

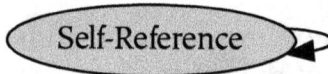

Figure 2.4.4c: A self-reference refers to itself.

A common example of self-reference is the *Liar's Paradox*, attributed to Parmenides (ca. 485 BCE):

I am lying.

---

[37] This does not entail that ultimate referents are *independently* meaningful: they may contribute only a portion of meaning, and/or derive their meaning from part/whole relations with other referents. However, the meaning of an ultimate referent cannot be entirely referential.

Although this statement seems rather innocuous at first, its truth or falsity is difficult to assess. If it is assumed to be true, then it becomes false. At the point of being negated, it becomes true once again. Establishing the ultimate validity of this sentence is therefore impossible, as it involves an infinite regress.

Probably the most significant thing about Parmenides' statement is that it is self-referential: it describes itself. Hence, a reasonable first step in the elimination of paradoxes eliminates self-reference. Unfortunately, the recognition of self-reference is confounded because reference does not have to be *immediate*; it can be a multi-step, circular phenomena, as illustrated by the two statements below:

1. Statement (2) is true.
2. Statement (1) is false.

The paradox in this case is more difficult to spot, but it is an example of self-reference when both statements are considered as a single whole that refers to itself.[38] Specifically, the first statement is neither true nor false until it is evaluated. If one assumes that it is true, the truth of the second statement is asserted. The second statement asserts that the first statement is false, which contradicts the original assumption, and so on, such that the truth conditions never converge.

2.4.4.4 Empty References
Empty references refer to nothing.

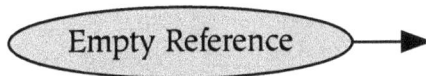

Figure 2.4.4d: An empty reference does not refer to anything.

---

[38] In other words, these two statements entail self-reference when seen as a whole from a larger perspective. As a result, they create a cycle which prevents the referential space in which they occur from being well-ordered.

Although almost all referential relations involve a referent, there is one important exception: the empty reference, which is a reference whose referent does not exist or which refers to *nothing*. Since it has no referent, it is not entirely clear that it is a reference, although it is widely used in practice.

2.4.4.5 Full References

Full references refer to everything.

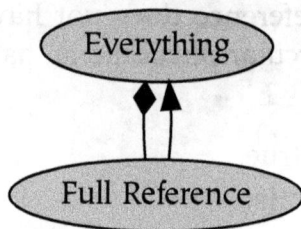

Figure 2.4.4e: A full reference refers to everything.

Another unusual type of reference that bears mention is the full reference, which refers to *everything*, or to all things at the referential level to which it refers. It is particularly significant because it forms a trivial isomorphism between two referential levels (i.e., because it refers to all referents at a given referential level, it does not require any discrimination to be learned between those referents).

The full reference is defined constructively, or in virtue of things that exist at a lower referential level. As an important side effect, a full reference never refers to itself. This definition avoids the paradoxes associated with self-reference by using a (constructivist) solution identical to that proposed for similar conundrums related to the set of all sets.

Chapter 5
Combining Spaces

The combination of mereological and referential spaces yields spaces unlike either one.

Most of this book uses <u>hierarchies</u> to structure spaces because of their relative simplicity. Hierarchies are a structure whose nodes are described using the metaphor of a family tree: parents are depicted above children and siblings are depicted next to one another. Hierarchy can also be described using the tree metaphor, although the trees are typically depicted as branching downwards instead of upwards, such that parent and child nodes are called "root" and "branch" nodes.

Different types of hierarchies use different structuring elements as relations. This chapter examines the two different types of hierarchies that correspond most closely to mereological and referential spaces: meronomies and taxonomies.

2.5.1 Meronomies

Meronomies are hierarchies that are structured with the composition relation.

Meronomies are mereological hierarchies in which the children are *parts* of the parent. Meronomies simultaneously represent divisions of a larger whole and collections of parts, so if the trunk *is-a-part-of* the tree then the tree *is-a-whole-of* the trunk, and vice-versa. Figure 2.5.1a depicts the meronomy of a tree, whose parts are   roots, trunk, branches, and leaves. It depicts those parts using the *composition* relation, which is often called the *has-a* relation, as in "a tree has-a trunk".

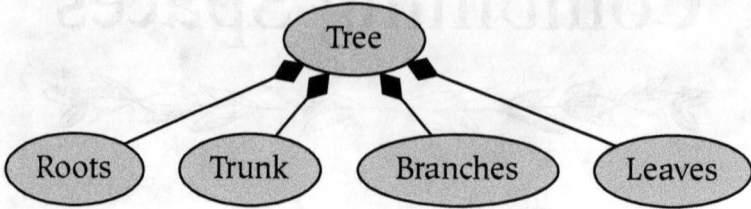

Figure 2.5.1a: A meronomy is a hierarchy that uses the composition relation.

It is not possible to create meronomies with abstract child nodes; the rationale behind this is based on their cognitive structure, and is discussed in section *Cognitive Taxonomies* (p. 102). Therefore, even though it is true that a pine is a tree, a maple is a tree, and an elm is a tree, meronomies like those shown in Figure 2.5.1b are invalid (where the superscript "+" denotes that the entity is abstract).

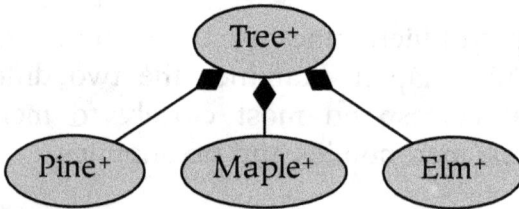

Figure 2.5.1b: A meronomy is invalid if its child nodes are abstract.

It is possible to create meronomies that have discontiguous concrete nodes, although they are somewhat uncommon (perhaps because it is easier to form concrete concepts of contiguous objects than of discontiguous objects). As an example, Figure 2.5.1c illustrates a whole ("All trees") that is composed of parts that are concrete collections of different trees ("All pines", "All maples", and "All elms").

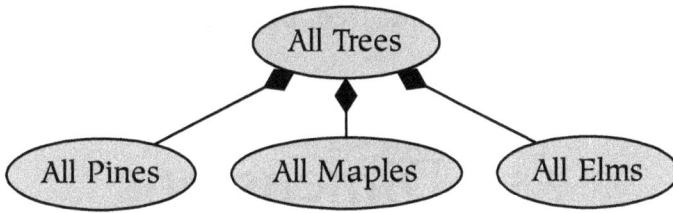

Figure 2.5.1c: A discontiguous meronomy.

2.5.2 Taxonomies

Taxonomies are hierarchies that are structured with the generalization relation.

Taxonomies are type hierarchies, in which the child things are *kinds* of the parent things. The primary difference between meronomies and taxonomies is that taxonomies are composed of abstract things: they are composed of types or classes of things rather than concrete things, and they entail the use of references (taxonomic construction is described in section *Cognitive Taxonomies*, p. 102).

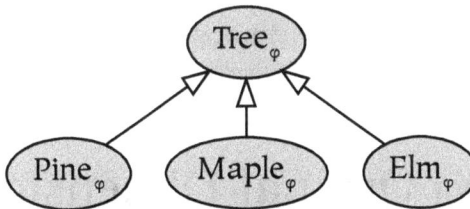

Figure 2.5.2: A taxonomy is a hierarchy that uses the generalization relation.

The taxonomy depicted in Figure 2.5.2 illustrates the abstract type *tree*, which is composed of three other types of things: *pines*, *maples*, and *elms* (where the subscript φ denotes that the entity is a concept). The empty triangle denotes the *generalization* relation, which is often called the *is-a* relation, as in "a pine is-a tree". In common English usage, the difference between meronomies and taxonomies is that a pine *is-a* tree, but a trunk *is-a-part-of-a* tree (or a tree *has-a* trunk).

2.5.3 Dimensions
*Dimensions are axes along which
a thing can be differentiated.*

Dimensions are the measurable extents of things in space. The number of dimensions of an object are the number that are necessary to specify a unique location within that space. Although physical dimensions are continuous, dimensions may in general correspond to several types of *scales*: ordinal, nominal, and interval (ratio scales are omitted for brevity). These types of scales correspond to sorted, unsorted, and measurable dimensions, as illustrated in the following examples:

♦ The order in which children arrive at the dinner table imposes an *ordinal* (sorted) dimension over those children.

♦ The names of children create a *nominal* (unsorted) dimension over those children.

♦ The ages of children impose an *interval* (measurable) dimension over those children.

2.5.3.1 Ordinal Dimensions
*Ordinal dimensions are sorted by a structural element such
as the composition relation.*

An ordinal dimension imposes a total or partial order on the elements that it structures. For example, finishing first, second, or third in a marathon are relative positions that constitute an ordinal dimension. Knowing the position does not tell you exactly what the finishing time was, but it does convey that one finishing time is greater or lesser than another.

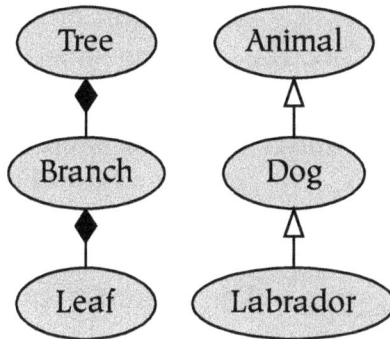

Figure 2.5.3a: Ordinal dimensions sort their elements.

Two different ordinal relationships are shown in Figure 2.5.3a. Because parts must be smaller than wholes, an *order* is established between the nodes labeled "tree", "branch", and "leaf". Ordinal relations are transitive: if a leaf is a part of a branch, and a branch is a part of a tree, then a leaf is a part of a tree. Similarly, if a Labrador is a dog, and a dog is an animal, then a Labrador is an animal. As the diagram illustrates, an ordinal dimension imposes an order which is not present among siblings (e.g., there is no order between different types of animals such as dogs and cats).

2.5.3.2 Nominal Dimensions

Nominal dimensions are constituted by unordered entities, which are distinguished only by name.

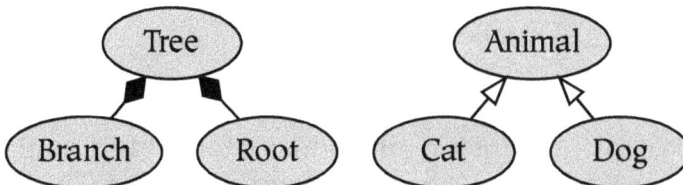

Figure 2.5.3b: Nominal dimensions name their elements.

A nominal dimension is unordered, since it has no basis to determine the relative positions of things. Figure 2.5.3b depicts two such dimensions, parts of trees and types of animals, both of which are nominal because the position of the child nodes is not significant (and therefore the children must be distinguished by name).

For taxonomies, nominal dimensions create <u>nominal identity</u>. Nominal identity works by creating a parent type that contains all of the children as subtypes or tokens, which become identical with respect to being tokens of that type (in this way, the children form an <u>equivalence class</u>). For example, cats and dogs are the same to the extent that they are both animals.[39] Nominal identity is explored further in section *Wholes of References* (p. 47).

2.5.3.3 Interval Dimensions

Interval dimensions are formed by combining nominal and ordinal dimensions.

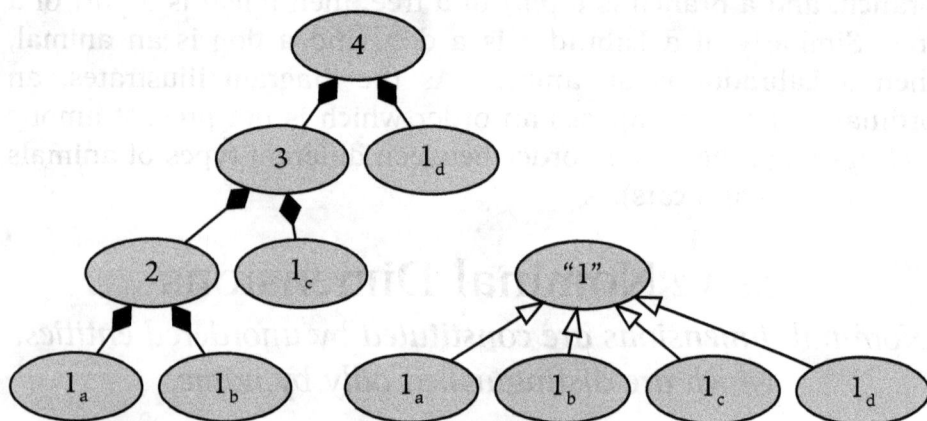

Figure 2.5.3c: Interval dimensions combine ordinal and nominal dimensions.

An interval dimension introduces an additional relation between its parts that results in a measurable distance (or metric) between those parts. A numerical example is shown in Figure

---

[39] Although it sounds odd to say that a cat is a dog, it is also odd to say that one cat is another, or even that a middle-aged cat is the *same* cat as that cat when it was a kitten.

2.5.3c, where 1 is the same distance from 2 as 2 is from 3 and as 3 is from 4, precisely because the distance from one to the next is the *same* number (1). Since the *same* node cannot appear more than once in a meronomy, the meronomy on the left depicts the repeated unit element (1) as different things (1_n). These different things form an equivalence class in the taxonomy on the right, however, which is what makes the intervals identical (i.e., all "1").

2.5.4 Orthogonality

Two dimensions are orthogonal if a change in one dimension does not necessitate a change in the other.

When working with multiple dimensions, it is useful to characterize them with respect to one another as being either dependent or independent. If dimensions are independent of one another, they are called <u>orthogonal</u>. For example:

◆ The colors and sizes of an object form orthogonal dimensions, since you can change the color of an object without changing its size (and vice-versa).

◆ The size and weight of a thing are not orthogonal, since the size of an object is correlated to its weight (assuming constant density).

◆ Euclidean dimensions are orthogonal to each other, because you can change the position of an object on the x-axis without changing its position on the y-axis.

Diagrammatically, orthogonality determines how hierarchies can be combined with one another. For example, assume that one wishes to combine the two taxonomies shown in Figure 2.5.4a, which divide a common type (*x*) into subtypes *a*, *b*, *c*, and *d*. These hierarchies can be combined in two primary ways: either by grafting parent nodes together or by appending the branches of one hierarchy to each of the terminal nodes of the other. The criteria for choosing one method as opposed to the other is both to prevent <u>overlap</u> of the nodes and to ensure that the space is fully partitioned.

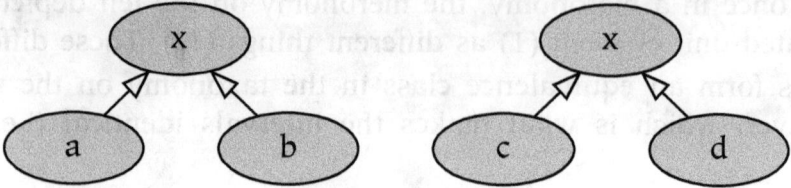

Figure 2.5.4a: Two hierarchies representing different divisions of the same whole.

The first possibility for combining these two taxonomies is to create a single tree with a parent (x) and four child nodes (a, b, c, and d). For example, if the a/b and c/d distinctions both correspond to color, and no object can have multiple colors, then the two dependent hierarchies are combined, as in Figure 2.5.4b. When the a/b and c/d dimensions are orthogonal, however, this type of combination is not appropriate. For example, if the a/b dimension represents "young animals"/"old animals", and c/d represents "stupid animals"/"smart animals", then combining these dimensions in a flat hierarchy would not create a structure capable of categorizing animals that are both smart and young.

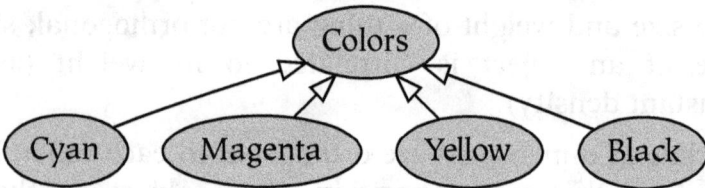

Figure 2.5.4b: A combined (1-D) hierarchy.

Therefore, combining hierarchies that are orthogonal requires appending the branches of one tree to each of the terminal nodes of the other tree, as shown in Figure 2.5.4c. This kind of combination increases the depth of the hierarchy, and that additional depth allows additional information to be encoded. Each of the four different choices corresponds to a path from the root of the tree to a terminal node, or a selection from each of the two constituent categorizations, young/old and smart/stupid. As a result, the previous dilemma of how to categorize smart young animals is resolved (and corresponds to the rightmost path in the tree).

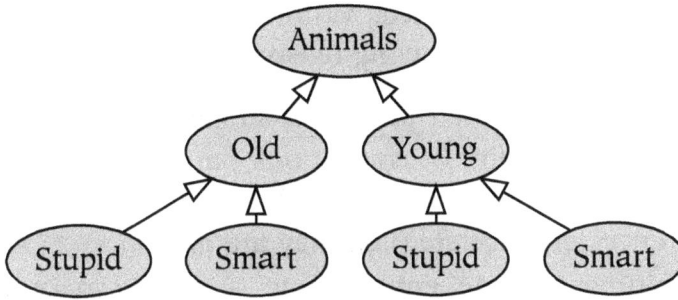

Figure 2.5.4c: A combined (2-D) hierarchy.

2.5.5 Wholes of References

Wholes of references are wholes of parts that are also references in a referential space.

In mereological space, things can be both wholes and parts. In referential space, things can be both references and referents. The combination of mereological and referential spaces results in further subtypes:

- Wholes that are references
- Wholes that are referents
- Parts that are references
- Parts that are referents

The arbitrary combination of wholes, parts, referents, and references in the context of cognition is not always useful, however, since many of these combinations do not exist. For example, it is not possible to form parts of references, so that combination is not explored further. It is possible, however, to form wholes-of-parts-that-are-references (or *wholes of references*), and that construct is widely used.

A whole of references exists within mereological space; however, each of the parts of that whole (i.e., the references) also exist within referential space. Wholes of references are unlike wholes of parts for the following reasons:

1. Wholes combine their parts in a single space.
2. The dimensionality of continuous parts is equivalent to the dimensionality of their wholes.
3. References are discrete (i.e., they are atoms).
4. Combining discrete entities into a single space creates a discrete space whose dimensionality is one higher than its constituent referential atoms (i.e., since combining discrete entities in a single space is not possible without doing so).

In a cognitive context, wholes of references are called *symbols*, which are explored further in section _Symbolic Space_ (p. 91). For now, it is sufficient to note that wholes of references are the basis of *generalization* (the operation used to construct taxonomies). Therefore, wholes of references are the basis of nominal identity (i.e., two things are nominally identical if they are <u>tokens</u> of the same <u>type</u>, as explored in section _Nominal Dimensions_, p. 43.

2.5.6 Beyond Hierarchy

Hierarchies are a pragmatic but limited structure
for comprehending reality.

Although hierarchies are useful and relatively easy to grasp conceptually, there are several problems associated with the reification of hierarchies:

1. Hierarchies have only one root, which reinforces the notion that all parts have a single whole.

2. Hierarchies do not have overlapping nodes; therefore, they implicitly reinforce the notion that there is a single correct way to partition reality.

3. Because a single hierarchy categorizes things in only one way, objects are often identified exclusively as parts, wholes, references, referents, or some combination thereof.

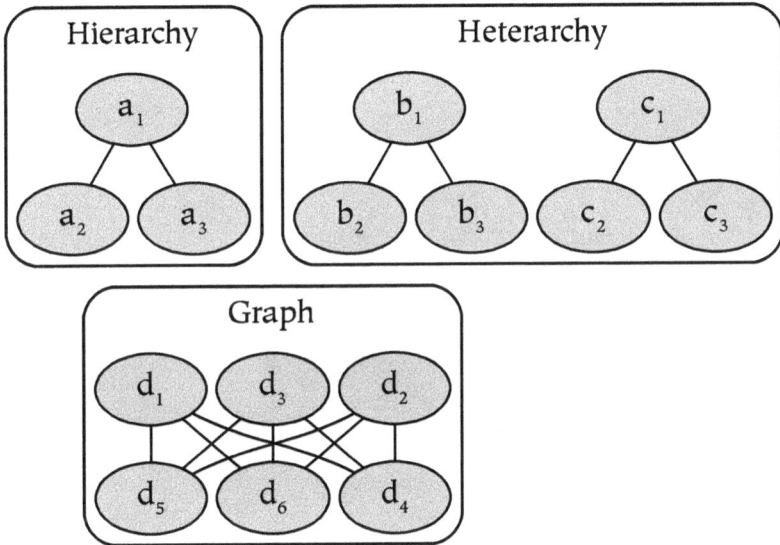

Figure 2.5.6: Three different ways to organize nodes.

Two alternatives to hierarchies are presented in Figure 2.5.6: heterarchies and graphs. Although these alternatives are comparatively less simplistic, neither of them addresses the complexity of multiple overlapping layers and nodes. To partially address this lack, bidirectional parthood (overlap) and bidirectional reference are introduced in appendix *Ideographic Conventions* (p. 214).

2. Hierarchies do not have overlapping nodes; therefore, they implicitly reinforce the notion that there is a single correct way to partition reality.

3. Because a single hierarchy categorizes things in only one way, objects are often identified exclusively as parts, wholes, reference, referents, or some combination thereof.

Figure 2.5. Three different ways to organize nodes.

Two alternatives to hierarchies are presented in Figure 2.5.6: hierarchies and graphs. Although these alternatives are comparatively less simplistic, neither of them addresses the complexity of multiple overlapping layers and nodes. To partially address this issue, bidirectional parenthood (overlap) and bidirectional reference are introduced in appendix 2 Ideographic Conventions, p. 214).

Part 3

THE BASIC MODEL

Applying the theory of mereology and reference to human experience creates physical, subjective, and conceptual spaces, as well as several relations between those spaces.

The basic model of cognition begins with the <u>universe</u>, or *physical space*, and defines two further subspaces from the perspective of an individual. Everything within physical space that is experienced by that individual constitutes *subjective space*, and everything within subjective space that is conceptualized by that individual constitutes *conceptual space*. In summary:

♦ **Physical space (U)** is the physical universe, or reality. Its parts are called *events*.

♦ **Subjective space (S)** is everything in physical space that is experienced by a given individual. Its parts are called *experiences*.

♦ **Conceptual space (C)** is everything in subjective space that is conceptualized by that individual. Its parts are called *concepts*.

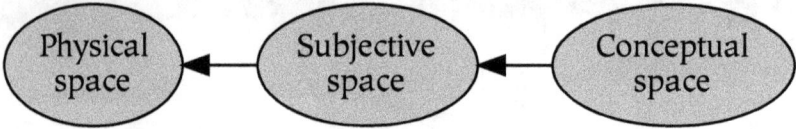

Figure 3a: Three referential spaces.

These spaces are distinguished in terms of reference: subjective space contains references to physical space, and conceptual space contains references to subjective space. Because the notion of reference in a psychological context corresponds to knowing, they are called *epistemic spaces*. For example, for a concept to reference an object is for it to know about (or represent) that object. Therefore, minds are collections of references, in addition to whatever else they may be.

These epistemic spaces can be depicted in virtue of their referential or reflective relationship to one another, as in Figure 3a. These spaces are also parts of one another: subjective space is a part of physical space and conceptual space is a part of subjective space. This is graphically depicted in Figures 3b and 3c, both of which express the same thing.

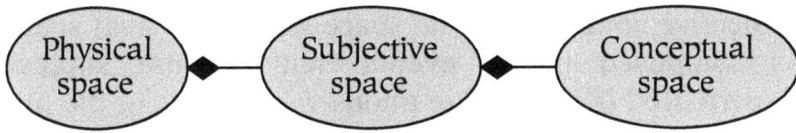

Figure 3b: Depicting spaces as parts
of one another.

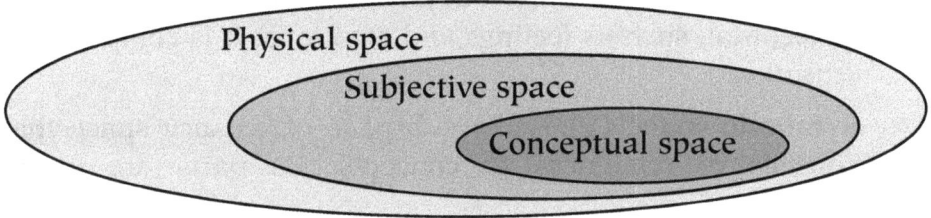

Figure 3c: Depicting spaces contained
within one another.

Using the second type of notation (<u>UML</u>), these three spaces can also be depicted as referential parts of each other, as in Figure 3d.

Figure 3d: Three spaces as referential parts.

When these spaces are viewed as parts of one another, the complements of those parts with respect to their wholes creates two further spaces, *objective space* and *sensory space*.[40] By definition, therefore, objective space is not sensed (**O=U-S**) and sensory space is not conceptualized (**N=S-C**). It is also useful to distinguish a symbolic space that is a specialized part of sensory space, the parts of which are symbols that reference concepts. These three further spaces may be summarized as follows:

---

[40] Note that objective space is only objective from the point of view of a particular individual, so it may overlap with the subjective space of a different individual.

◆ **Objective space (O)** is the space within physical space that is composed of all events that are not subjectively experienced (i.e., they are unobserved events in the physical universe, independent of the observer). Its parts are called *objects*.

◆ **Sensory space (N)** is the space within a subjective space that is composed of all subjective experience that is not conceptual, such as feelings and emotions. It is composed of *sensation*.

◆ **Symbolic space (V)** is the subspace of sensory space that consists of references to concepts. Its parts are called *symbols*.

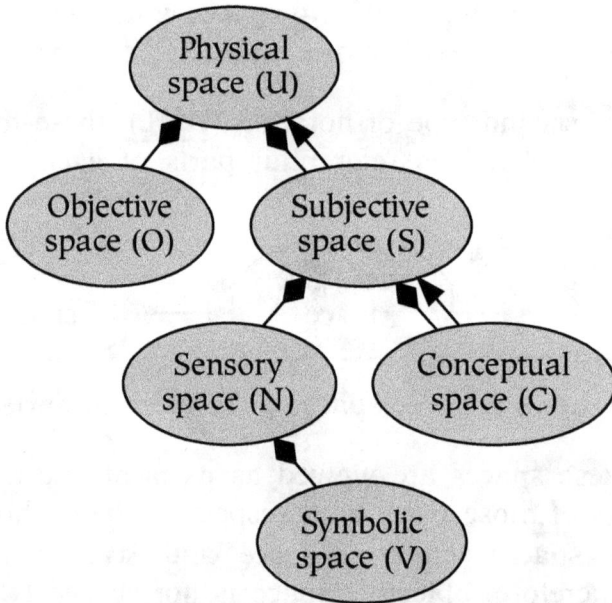

Figure 3e: The six spaces (U, O, S, N, C, V), shown as referential parts of one another.

Diagrammatically, all six spaces are depicted in Figure 3e. The objective (O), sensory (N), and conceptual (C) spaces, and the relations between them, form the basis for the basic model of cognition that is used throughout the book. They form a partition of physical space that is defined by two dichotomies: the subjective/objective dichotomy and the sensory/conceptual dichotomy.

The subjective/objective dichotomy is the basis for two important relations, sensation and action:[41]

◆ **Sensation (Θ)** causes experiences in subjective space as a result of objects in objective space.

◆ **Action (Δ)** causes or changes objects in objective space as a result of subjective experiences.

These relations are depicted in the context of objective and subjective space in Figure 3f. As a model of cognition, this corresponds closely to behaviorism, although *stimulus* and *response* are replaced with the more humanistic terms *sensation* and *action*. Further, the model developed here presents subjective space as a mind with a subjective point of view, rather than as an object or animal.

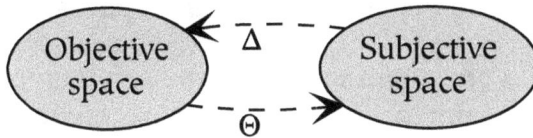

**Figure 3f: The relations between
the subjective and objective spaces.**

The sensory/conceptual dichotomy divides subjective space into conceptual and nonconceptual subspaces, which is represented in Figure 3g. As mentioned, subjective space consists of references to physical space. Within subjective space, the relations of the references between the conceptual and sensory

---

[41] Cognitive mereological and referential relations are depicted with Greek letters and dashed arrows rather than with diamond and triangle arrowheads, since they only constitute parts and wholes *from the subjective perspective*. In other words, conceptual and sensory spaces are not necessarily physical parts of one another, even though concepts are *subjectively experienced* as wholes of sensation.

spaces represent the mereological and referential relations of objects in the world.

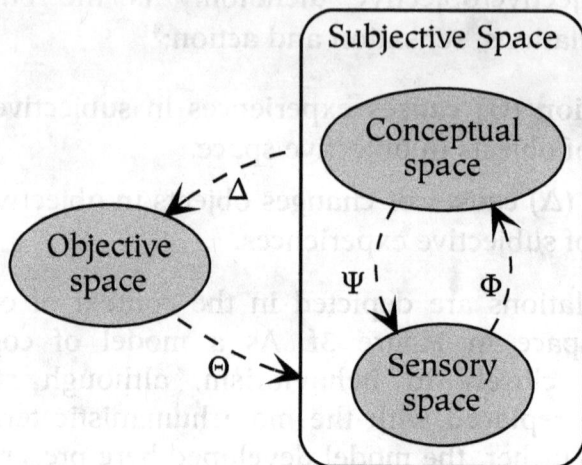

Figure 3g: Dividing subjective space into sensory and conceptual spaces.

Sensory and conceptual spaces, although they are modeled as discrete entities, form a continuum whose content is sensation, and which is collected into increasingly large conceptual wholes as one moves from sensory space to conceptual space.[42] Movement in the opposite direction is also possible, which entails creating increasingly sensory perceptual parts from conceptual wholes. These two operations are called *conceptualization* and *visualization*, respectively. Conceptualization and visualization correspond to the mereological operations of whole and part:

---

[42] The basic model of cognition allows wholes of wholes and parts of parts, although for simplicity, they are not depicted as a transition (i.e., from sensory space to conceptual space).

- **Conceptualization (Φ)** is an act of whole-making, which creates concepts out of sensation.

- **Visualization (Ψ)** is an act of part-making, which creates sensation out of concepts.

In addition to these mereological relations corresponding to whole and part, there are two referential relations which capture symbolic relations between conceptual and sensory space (or more specifically, between conceptual and symbolic space):

- **Interpretation (Ω)** is an act that dereferences a symbol and activates its associated concept.

- **Symbolization (Ξ)** is an act that references a concept and activates its associated symbol.

These two relations associate concepts and symbols, and thus map between conceptual space and symbolic space. Because symbols are modeled as sensations with symbolic meaning, the symbolic space that they form is a subspace of sensory space. Hence, symbols are significantly different from concepts; while concepts provide understanding in virtue of being wholes of sensory content, symbols are representations that correspond to words and enable language and thought (symbols are explored further in section _Symbolic Space_, p. 91).

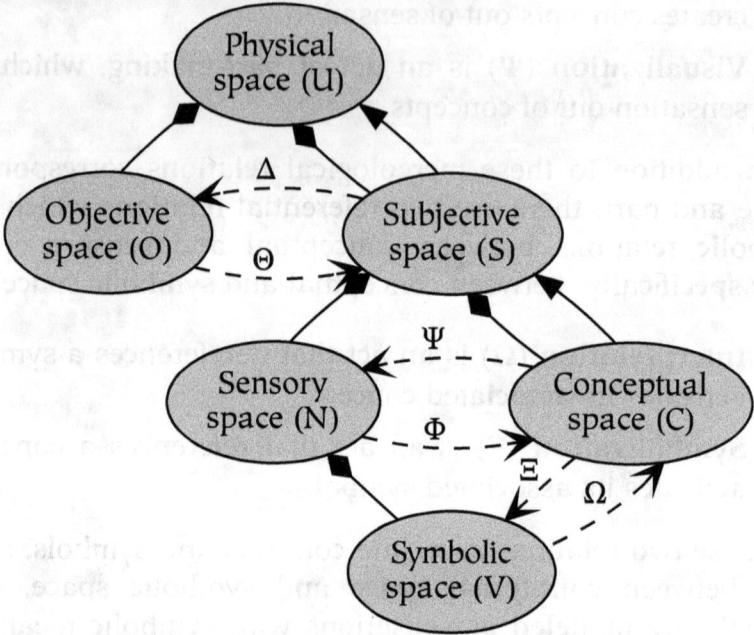

Figure 3h: The basic model in full detail, with relations: sensation (Θ), action (Δ), conceptualization (Φ), visualization (Ψ), interpretation (Ω), and symbolization (Ξ).

Combining Figures 3e and 3g and adding the interpretation and symbolization relations yields the model shown in Figure 3h.

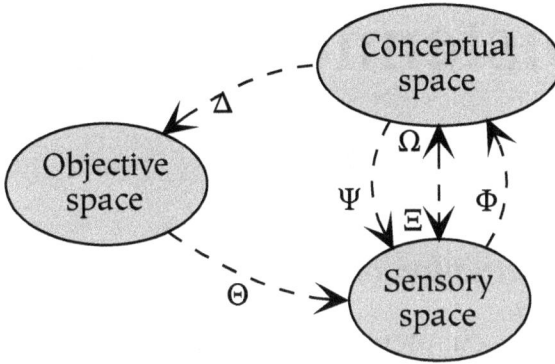

Figure 3i: The basic model of cognition.

In the interest of simplicity, however, this diagram is reduced to the *basic model of cognition* shown in Figure 3i. The three nodes represent mutually-exclusive spaces, and the edges (or dashed arrows) depict the flow of information between those nodes.

Chapter 6
Epistemic Universes

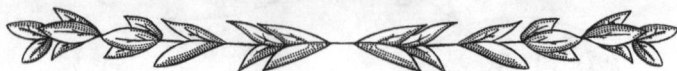

A presentation of three epistemic universes.

The next three chapters examine the physical, subjective, and conceptual spaces consecutively. Since each space is boundless from its own point of view, they are also referred to as universes. For example, the subjective universe is a complete whole or totality in so far as all things can be experienced, and a given individual can never have experience outside of it. Similarly, conceptual space is also a universe in that all things can be conceptualized.[43] That said, they are universes determined by the subjective perspective, so things that form a subjective universe from one point of view do not do so from another.

For clarity, it is important to explicitly specify the intended epistemic space of things that exist in multiple epistemic spaces. For example, the idea of an orange, the sensation of an orange, and the orange itself must be carefully distinguished from each other. Therefore, this book follows a convention for referring to the different types of entities as that is depicted in the taxonomy of Figure 3.6a, where the root node (a *thing*) is a generic type that can be used in any epistemological space, and its subtypes are scoped to each subsequent epistemic space (which mirrors the spaces as depicted in Figure 3e).

---

[43] To use a more concrete example, our house may be a part of the world which we enter and leave, but if we never leave it, it is our sensory universe. People may come and visit, and tell us about the world outside, and we may form an *idea* of the universe outside, but we still form that idea *from within our house*.

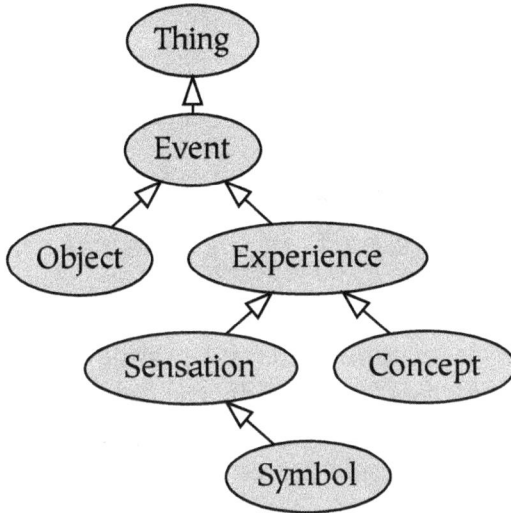

Figure 3.6a: The types of things within each epistemic space.

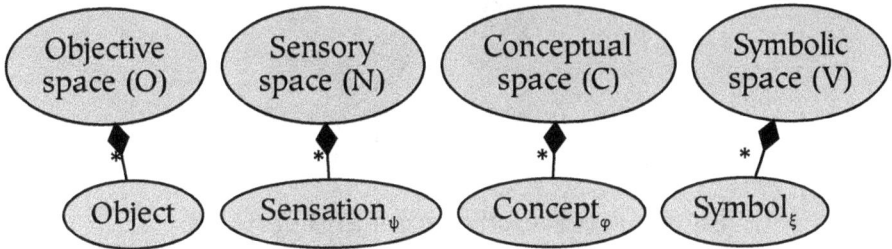

Figure 3.6b: The parts of objective, sensory, conceptual, and
symbolic spaces are respectively known as
objects, sensations, concepts, and symbols.

Epistemic types corresponding to four of those spaces are illustrated in Figure 3.6b.[44] The subscripts (or lack thereof) designate their associated entities as either <u>objects</u>, <u>sensations</u>, <u>concepts</u>, or <u>symbols</u>. For example, orange$_\varphi$ refers to the concept

---

[44] The combination of sensation and conceptualization is referred to as perception. Similarly, concepts in conjunction with their sensory content are known as percepts.

of an orange (for more details, see appendix *Typographical Conventions*, p. 212).

3.6.1 The Physical Universe
All events are parts of the physical universe.

The physical universe includes everything from the physical point of view.[45] It occupies the full range of every dimension which is attributed to it, including the temporal. It contains all things as events, which form parts of it. Even minds are a part of the universe, whether minds are equated with brains or subjective experience. Thus from the objective point of view, sensations and concepts are kinds of objects (i.e., they have a physical realization).

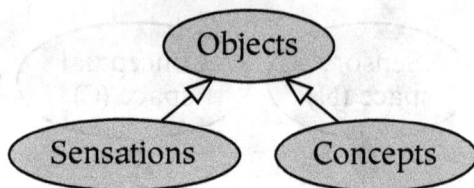

Figure 3.6.1: Sensations and concepts depicted as types of objects.

3.6.1.1 Objective Parts
The parts of objective space are called objects.

What are the primitives of reality? Are there things out of which reality is composed, such that there is a unique decomposition into certain parts and not others? Or if the world may be both conceptually and physically partitioned in numerous

---

[45] This implies that even mental phenomena are physical, in addition to whatever else they may be. In other words, what is *subjective* from one point of view is *objective* from another point of view.

different ways, is it at least possible to characterize which *types* of things constitute valid parts?

One way to answer the question about which types of things exist relies on the dimensionality of those things. For example, the theory called *presentism* maintains that physical things are 3-D entities that arise and pass away each instant. The theory called *eternalism* posits that physical things are 4-D entities that have an inherent temporal aspect, of which only a temporal slice is perceived.[46]

If one subscribes to the theory that objects share the dimensionality of the objective universe, then the dimensionality of space is a deciding factor in these deliberations.[47] For example, if the universe only exists at one time, then it contains only objects that exist entirely within the present, and not objects that have a temporal extent. Similarly, if the universe is temporally extended and at least 4-D, then the objects within it are also at least 4-D. For example, if a bike ride is 4-D, then the parts of that bike ride (such as the start, middle, and finish of the bike ride) are also 4-D events; as the bicycle itself is not a 4-D part, it does not exist as a concrete or real entity.

For most people, treating objects as 4-D things entails a shift in both mental perspective and verbal behavior. For example, 4-D things are not alterable or mutable: only objects *without* a temporal extent can undergo change over time. Expressed slightly differently, if 4-D objects do change, they must change in a dimension other than the four which serve to define them as objects. Further, if 4-D objects are concrete, then 3-D objects are abstract, a notion that runs counter to the current predominant worldview.[48]

---

[46] 4-D entities are also called *occurrents* (see [Simmons, 2000]).

[47] To support the theoretical position that all parts of the physical universe share its dimensionality, the relationship of N-D objects to several experiments in modern physics is explored in the essays section of [http://thewholepart.com].

[48] For example, the distinction between abstract and concrete in 3-D space is the distinction between "child" vs "my child", where "child" is seen as a

3.6.1.2 Objective Dimensions
The objective dimensions form a conditional space.

To examine objective space, it is necessary to take a perspective which is outside of any particular subjectivity, or which is valid from within every subjective perspective. In order to do that, objective truths form a set of relative *laws*. These universal laws take the form of conditional propositions, or experiments whose validity can be tested. If the statements are valid for everyone, then they are objectively true. This underscores an important fact about dimensionality: the number of dimensions of physical space is inferred from the number of dimensions that are used to formulate its physical laws.

The Number of Objective Dimensions
There are at least four physical dimensions.

The universe is often defined as "everything that exists", which is slightly misleading in that it denotes only the present moment. In particular, *what is current* turns out to be subjective; the sequence of separate events in 3-D space depends on the observer's frame of reference, and is not the same for all observers. Therefore, the Euclidean concept of an extended 3-D space that exists at a single time is untenable: there is no *single time* for all positions. A spacetime consisting of at least four dimensions is necessary for a model of objective space that is valid for all observers and which does not depend on subjective reference point.[49]

The necessity of four dimensions, however, does not entail an upper limit; the dimensionality that is ascribed to space grows as

---

general type and "my child" is seen as a specific instance of that type. However, in a 4-D space, "my child" is actually an abstraction, of which "my child on Tuesday" is a (more) concrete instance. For further discussion, see [Ingram and Tallant, 2018] or [Markosian, 2016].

[49] The notion that space is 4-D, or that time is an integral part of space, was proposed by Hermann Minkowski in 1908. Therefore, spacetime is more formally known in physics as Minkowski space.

necessary to accommodate the physical equations that are used. On a practical level, the number of dimensions may be limited by the number required to change from one subjective reference frame to another, since that is all that it takes to make different observations agree with one another. Although the equations that express physical laws such as relativity are easily expressed in 4-D spaces, some theories of physics such as string theory use ten or more dimensions, while people from <u>Flatland</u> get along with only two. On a theoretical level, there is no reason to posit any particular upper bound; space has as many dimensions as are used to describe it. Therefore, the physical universe is characterized as <u>open-dimensional</u>.[50]

The Nature of Objective Dimensions
The physical dimensions are usually described
as Euclidean and continuous.

Do the physical dimensions extend infinitely in all directions, or are they finite? Are they continuous and infinitely divisible, or are they discrete? Most people are either implicitly or explicitly committed to Euclidean dimensions, or to dimensions that extend in <u>orthogonal</u> directions from an arbitrarily assigned origin. This basis for constructing dimensionality is probably the simplest possibility, so it is adopted here.[51]

---

[50] Physical laws can be expressed in spaces of arbitrary dimensionality as well as other coordinate systems. For example, a two-dimensional coordinate could be expressed using two real numbers and a Euclidean coordinate system, such as the point at [y=1 inch, x=1 inch]. However, the same point in space could be located in a number of different ways; using polar coordinates, it would be specified as [angle=45 degrees, radius=1.414 inches].

[51] One alternative to Euclidean dimensions are spherical dimensions (or in the N-dimensional case, hyperspherical dimensions). To visualize a 2-D spherical space, imagine that you are an ant traveling on the surface of a sphere. If you go far enough in a given direction, even though you are traveling in a straight line with respect to the surface, you will end up where you started.

To ask if space continues infinitely is equivalent to asking if it is bounded, or if it is an *ultimate whole*. As discussed previously, boundaries are paradoxical if they are used as endpoints to finite spaces, because the nature of boundaries is to divide things, and one-sided endpoints do not provide two sides to divide. Therefore, space is most often understood as without any boundary and extending infinitely.

Just as the spatial extent of the universe may extend infinitely, so may its temporal extent. Finite temporal boundaries are known as moments of creation or destruction. These two temporal endpoints are not always regarded in the same way; for example, some people believe the temporal dimension extends infinitely in only one direction. Physicists generally believe in a beginning of time called *the big bang*, yet debate about whether time will have an ultimate end (which they call *the big collapse*). In non-European cultures, non-linear views of time are more prevalent. For example, members of the North American Hopi tribe see time as circular, while the Indian Vedic tradition envisions epochs of time as recurring perpetually.

Space itself is generally regarded as infinitely divisible and thus continuous, although there is some controversy about the continuity of matter in modern theories of quantum physics (further details about topological continuity are presented in appendix *Formal Summary*, p. 177).

3.6.2 The Subjective Universe

The subjective universe is the part of the physical universe that is experienced by an individual.

Although subjective space is only a part of the physical universe, it is *everything* from the subjective point of view. Only through subjective experience can one learn about the objective world: a world independent of experience, in which objects persist independently of any observation of them. In this respect, this work follows an inverted development by beginning with the physical universe.[52]

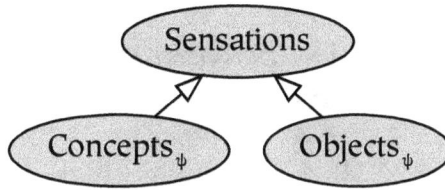

Sensations

Concepts$_\psi$ Objects$_\psi$

Figure 3.6.2a: Sensations of concepts and objects, depicted as types of sensations.

The subjective universe consists of both sensation and conceptualization; this chapter focuses on sensation, since it is epistemically prior to conceptualization (which is addressed in the next chapter). The term "sensation" as used in this context covers all nonconceptual experience; for example, even emotions are sensed, even though the sensation of emotions is quite different from the sensation of external phenomena. Thus, from the sensory point of view, objects$_\psi$ and concepts$_\psi$ are kinds of sensations (i.e., all things may be sensed).[53]

---

[52] This choice is a partial endorsement of the claim that "if a tree were to fall in the woods and no one was there to hear it, it *would* make a sound". Those who believe that there is no objective domain above and beyond the many subjective domains of individual experience may wish to substitute the term "multi-subjective universe" for the term "physical universe".

[53] Contrary to this hypothesis, there is some evidence that concepts cannot be sensed because there is no feeling within the brain (i.e., the brain lacks sensory neurons such as nociceptors). In either case, the symbols that reference concepts can be perceived.

3.6.2.1 The Subjective/Objective Dichotomy

The referential division between subjective/objective is similar to the mereological division between body/world.

A subjective space is defined as the part of the physical universe that is experienced by some individual. In virtue of this, the subjective perspective is localized in both space and time. One learns about objective space in virtue of both direct experience with the world and cultural transmission. For example, during the stage of development known as object permanence, children learn that there are objects that are not experienced, but which still exist (i.e., in objective space). These objects collectively form objective space, and are the complement of subjective space with respect to the physical universe. In virtue of these two spaces, the subjective/objective dichotomy is formed.

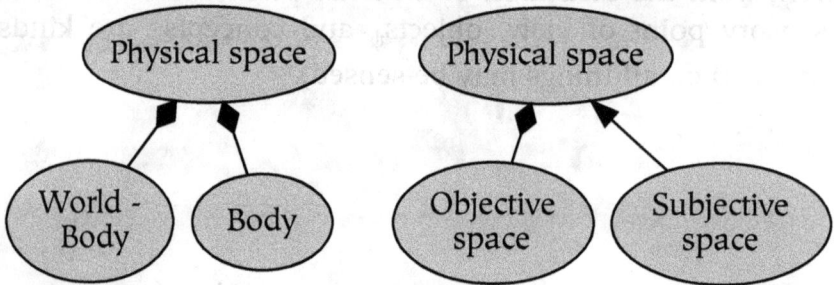

Figure 3.6.2b: Physical space can be divided mereologically (as body/world) and referentially (as subjective/objective).

The subjective/objective dichotomy is very different from the body/world dichotomy (where "world" in this context means the world with that particular body excluded). By definition, the subjective/objective boundary is determined referentially, while the body/world boundary is determined mereologically. As a consequence, if someone does not sense the hair on the back of their head, then it is not a part of their subjective space, even though it is a part of their body. Conversely, the hair that someone sees on the back of someone else's head *is* a part of their subjective space, though it clearly is not a part of their body.

These two dichotomies within physical space greatly influence how people define the self/other dichotomy. This dichotomy is most often characterized as creating non-overlapping parts of a larger whole, which is more closely aligned with a mereological definition than with a referential definition. Perhaps the self, when understood as a collection of parts that are references, is more easily identified with parts than with references. This bias may occur because parts are a necessary prerequisite of references to parts, because of cultural transmission, or due to a legacy of language and thought that establishes the border between self and other as the border of the skin or nervous system.

From a subjective point of view, do we experience our references as things within us, or do we experience what our mental references reference, and therefore as objects outside of us? If we do experience our mind as outside of us, then to identify with that mind is to identify with objects beyond our skin, rather than with the mechanism that supports that experience. As an intuitive argument in support of this claim, it is somewhat odd to identify with something that is not experienced (such as bodily parts that are not sensed), and perhaps just as odd *not* to identify with what *is* sensed (such as the sensation of objects external to our body).

One reason to identify exclusively with bodily sensation as opposed to sensation in general is that bodily sensation is relatively stable when compared to the rapidly changing subjective universe. For example, turning one's head may change one's view in dramatic ways: it may rapidly move mountains into and out of sensory space. This relative impermanence is probably a principal reason why the experience of mountains is excluded from the self-concept; sensation corresponding to visual imagery of mountains is not consistent in comparison to bodily sensation.[54] In other words, the physical body offers more consistent sensation in virtue of stable proprioception; although the sensation of the body changes, it generally does so at a slower pace. So even though the subjective and objective spaces are defined to be exclusive of one another, their overlap across time is relatively much greater than that between body and world (e.g., which occurs in virtue of inhaling and exhaling).

3.6.2.2 Sensory Parts

The parts of sensory space are called sensations.

Sensation occurs in response to various internal and external objects. In general, the more sensation of an object, the better the detail and clarity of the perception. However, the atoms of sensation are not necessarily small. For example, a small object may be experienced as an intersection of relatively large sensory features such as color. In other words, a given sensation is partless because it is unanalyzed by us, not because it is a point.

Sensory space can be viewed as composed of many sensory parts, just as the objective world can be viewed as a collection of many objects. However, sensations form an unorganized feature space, and are only fully individuated and organized in a manner that corresponds to the world when they are collected into wholes by concepts.[55]

Taken together, sensation and conceptualization constitute perception. There are two basic theories about the directness of perception: <u>direct realism</u> maintains that objects are perceived directly and <u>indirect realism</u> maintains that only references to those objects are perceived. Since the parts of the subjective universe are understood as references to an external reality, the

---

[54] However, as Ralph Waldo Emerson said, "A foolish consistency is the hobgoblin of little minds, adored by little statesmen and philosophers and divines."

[55] Therefore, to represent sensations as *count nouns* is somewhat misleading, since the lack of individuation renders sensation more akin to a *mass noun* (or a substance without a form).

basic model of cognition at least partially endorses the latter view. This position is motivated by the observation that if perception is not experienced in virtue of subjective references, then there is no way to account for intersubjective perceptual differences. In other words, intersubjective perceptual differences such as hallucinations or the perception of beauty suggest that beings experience reality as subjectively filtered, as opposed to experiencing objective reality directly or non-referentially.[56]

That said, the distinction about the directness of perception may be a false dichotomy if it is possible to experience reality in both referential and non-referential ways (a thesis explored in section *Stratified Self*, p. 163). One reason for understanding this distinction as a forced choice is that the subjective/objective division is often defined as a single mereological or referential boundary, a definition which forces consciousness to be separate from the object of perception. On the other hand, at least some areas of consciousness such as the brain may be known both directly and indirectly, or both referentially and non-referentially.[57]

3.6.2.3 Sensory Dimensions

Sensation is open-dimensional and is typically partitioned into several internal and external modalities.

Traditionally, sensory space is divided according to modality, or in virtue of various specialized sense faculties. This division typically results in five external senses (smell, taste, touch,

---

[56] One might also argue that all aspects of reality can only exist in virtue of a subjective/objective interaction. For example, consider the way a single coin appears elliptical from one point of view and circular from another, which indicates that the coin itself is neither circular nor elliptical.

[57] The claim being made here is that individuals have simultaneous experience of multiple (overlapping) epistemic levels. This can be viewed as a psychological variant of the ontological claim that all of reality has both a relative and an absolute nature, a point argued by the Buddhist philosopher Shantideva.

hearing, and sight) and a number of internal senses (mental, emotional, and several others). In comparison to the external senses, the internal senses are not particularly well understood.[58] Presumably, this is because knowledge of internal senses relies more heavily on subjective experience that is unique to each individual, which is not available to intersubjective verification. Therefore, although internal sensations may be well known at an intuitive level, they are difficult to communicate about and often not conceptually well-organized.[59]

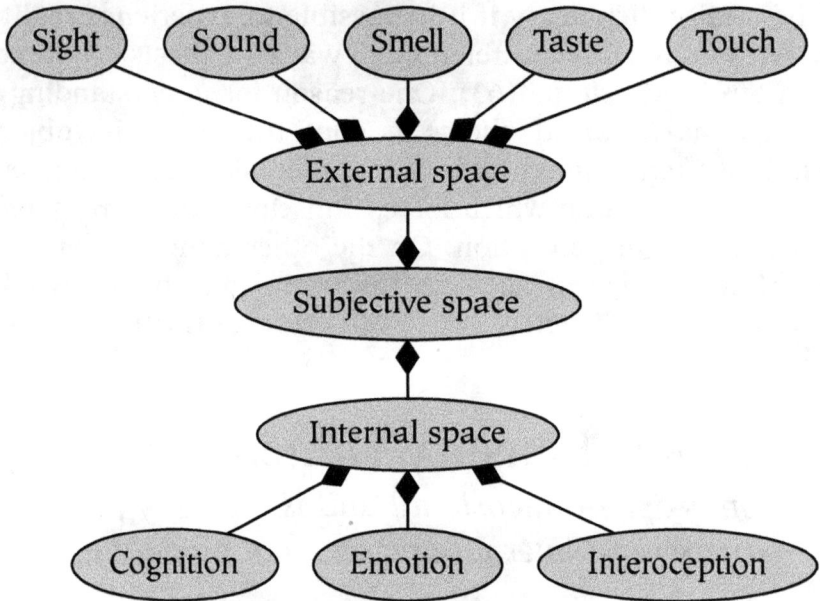

Figure 3.6.2c: Categorization of internal and external sensation.

---

[58] Evidence for this comes from the fact that the external senses have a fairly common categorization, while the internal senses do not. For example, there is no commonly agreed-upon categorization of human emotions.

[59] The science of subjectivity is difficult because of the inability to conceptualize and independently verify subjective experience. In other words, it is difficult to arrive at a consensus opinion about what is being referred to when talking about subjective experience because a given subjective domain does not present itself to multiple observers.

The Number of Sensory Dimensions
Sensory space is open-dimensional.

Concepts organize sensation into discrete units of perception (or <u>percepts</u>). Sensation itself is open-dimensional, and can be collected in arbitrary ways; in fact, dimensionality itself can be viewed as the result of a conceptual overlay on top of sensation. However, sensation can accommodate that conceptual overlay precisely because it supports discrimination; it is continuous.

The notion of an unstructured sensory space that is structured by concepts goes back at least to Kant, and probably earlier. In virtue of that conceptual structure, perception is guided by (top-down) attention. Carolyn Dicey-Jennings argues that it is attention which "transforms conscious experience from a pre-objective space to an objective space by invoking a common spatiotemporal framework" [Jennings, 2005], although the creation of that spatiotemporal framework is also to some degree hard-wired. For example, the dimensionality of visual sensation increases when moving posteriorly along the optic nerve, from sensation toward conceptuality. In particular, although sensation is 2-D when measured close to the retina of either eye, it becomes 3-D farther along the neural pathways, where the input from each eye is combined to determine the distance of a given object.[60]

The Nature of Sensory Dimensions
Sensory dimensions allow ordinal discrimination.

When sensation is conceptualized, it is initially individuated into percepts that are neither inherently small nor orthogonal. Even if those perceptual atoms correspond to individual neurons from the objective point of view, those neurons subjectively *reference* an aspect or region of the world that is often large and distributed, and which overlaps the aspects and regions of the world that are represented by other neurons. In other words,

---

[60] Since monocular vision does not provide information about the distance of an object, the input from each eye is combined neurally to form a disparity map, which is used to determine the distance of objects.

although minds can be physically divided into small material constituents such as neurons, those constituents are not small from a referential or subjective point of view. In fact, neurons often represent large-scale features such as color, edges, and linear orientation (and it is referential content that makes them meaningful from the subjective perspective). Therefore, sensation should not be identified with a set of points when viewed from the subjective perspective; rather, it should be considered as a number of arbitrarily large, *conceptually unanalyzed atoms*.

An important aspect of sensory space is that it supports discrimination. In particular, it must be possible even to discriminate sensations for which there are no concepts, since this discrimination forms the basis of conceptualization. As numerous psychophysical experiments demonstrate, the number of possible sensory discriminations is so large that sensory space can be regarded as continuous (for most purposes). Using the sensation of taste as an example, scientists claim that there are five dimensions of taste (sweet, bitter, sour, salty, and umami are reported in [Huang et al., 2006]). Assuming that one can discriminate twenty different intervals along each of the five dimensions of taste, that would create a space of 20^5 possible sensations, or more than three million different tastes.[61]

Another characteristic of sensory dimensions is that they are not linear with respect to the physical quantities that they represent. For example:

♦ The sensitivity to sound at high or low frequencies is lower than the sensitivity at the center of the audible range.

♦ The visual field is more sensitive to the intensity of light at

---

[61] In fact, twenty intervals grossly underestimates our discriminative capacity. In psychophysics, the lower limit of differentiation is called the *just noticeable difference*, which has been shown in studies of vision to be affected by the firing of a single neuron (see [Baylor & Lamb, 1979]).

the periphery than at the center.

♦ The sensation of touch is more acute at the fingers than at the forearms.

♦ The sensory input that is received from the fingers is greater than the input from the forearm (in terms of cortical area).[62]

Further, not only is cortical area disproportional to the bodily area that it represents, but that proportion changes over time. For example, if you take piano lessons, the size of the cortical area that is dedicated to your fingers will increase (an effect known as neuroplasticity). This can be taken as evidence (at least for those who believe in this sort of mind/brain correlation) that even the perception of a constant stimulus changes drastically throughout the course of our lives.

3.6.3 The Conceptual Universe

The conceptual universe is the part of the subjective universe that is conceptualized by an individual.

Although conceptual space is only a part of the subjective universe, it is *everything* from the conceptual point of view. Thus, from the conceptual point of view, objects$_\varphi$ and sensations$_\varphi$ are kinds of concepts (i.e., they have a conceptual realization).

Concepts are most often known in relation to one another. Therefore, knowing a concept entails knowing its mereological context within conceptual space, or knowing both its conceptual wholes and parts. For example, a tree stump is known as both a brown wooden thing in virtue of its brown parts, and as a tree of some particular species in virtue of its larger wholes. Similarly,

---

[62] Since fingers occupy a larger amount of sensory space than do our forearms based on the amount of cortex devoted to them, it seems reasonable to conclude that humans literally *sense more* of their fingers than of their forearms, even though fingers occupy a smaller amount of physical space.

the concept "water$_\varphi$" may be learned both via the sensation "water$_\psi$" and in terms of other concepts (e.g., "water$_\varphi$" is an abstract concept that belongs to the abstract concept "liquid$_\varphi$").

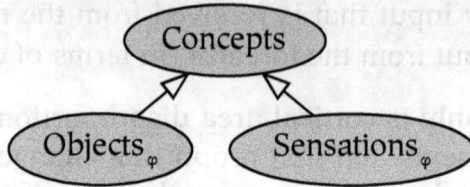

Figure 3.6.3a: Concepts of objects and sensations depicted as types of concepts.

3.6.3.1 The Sensory/Conceptual Dichotomy

The referential division between conceptual/perceptual is similar to the mereological division between brain/body.

The mereological body/brain dichotomy is analogous to the referential sensory/conceptual dichotomy. More precisely, the brain contains references that form conceptual space when they are subjectively experienced. Similarly, the body is approximately the location of the references which form sensory space when they are subjectively experienced.[63] The difference between these two is that the brain/body dichotomy treats references as non-referential physical entities, and the sensory/conceptual dichotomy treats references in virtue of their referential content. This can be informally summarized by saying that minds are located in brains from the third-person perspective, while brains are located in minds from the first-person perspective.

------

[63] There is an obvious disconnect in the analogy between "body" and "sensory space" in that sensory space extends referentially further than the body does mereologically. However, the body is the largest part of sensory space that is spatiotemporally contiguous or mereologically consistent, and thus easily named.

As with the subjective/objective dichotomy, sensory and conceptual spaces are defined without overlap. However, the boundary between what is sensed and what is conceptualized changes relatively more quickly, and therefore the overlap of content across time is much greater for the sensory/conceptual distinction than for the body/brain distinction.

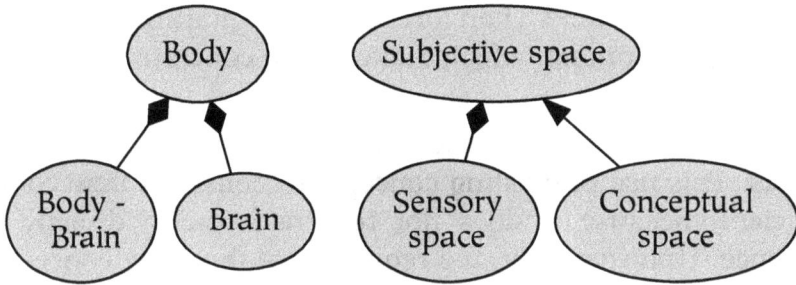

Figure 3.6.3b: The self can be divided mereologically (as brain/body) and referentially (as sensory/conceptual).

The sensory/conceptual dichotomy is a simplification of a continuum of perception that ranges from purely sensory content at one end to highly categorical and conceptual at the other (although the content itself does not change, since it is specified referentially).

Conceptual and sensory spaces overlap partially in virtue of visualization, a top-down process that strongly influences what is and what is not sensed. That doesn't mean that modalities such as thinking and seeing are the *same*, but that they both contribute to the same extended perceptual space; as a result, you can see what you are thinking. More precisely, if you are thinking, then you cannot see what you are *not* thinking (more detail about this difference is presented in section *Attention*, p. 140).

3.6.3.2 Conceptual Parts
The parts of conceptual space are called concepts.

Concepts can be categorized into two main types according to their composite structure: concepts composed of sensation and concepts composed of symbols. Concepts of sensation are called zeroth-order, and concepts of symbols are called higher-order. The distinction between zeroth-order concepts and higher-order concepts is similar to the distinction between Type 1 and Type 2 thought in the context of Dual Process Theory.

Because zeroth-order concepts are formed as wholes of sensation, the meaning of those concepts derives directly from that sensory content.[64] Therefore, they are guaranteed to have a spatiotemporal context, which makes them concrete.

Higher-order concepts, on the other hand, are higher in that they are composed of symbols which in turn reference other concepts. This use of existing concepts to construct new concepts is efficient, because it does not require learning directly from experience. Unfortunately, the requirement that new concepts are built using existing concepts entails a granularity that is not always a good fit for the object that is being represented. Further, in order to understand higher-order concepts, the sensory content of those constituent symbols must be visualized, which causes those concepts to be abstract.

As a result of the composite nature of higher order concepts, and in virtue of the top-down focus they require, such concepts are notoriously polarizing. For example, people often assert that a given conceptual proposition is entirely true or false, without allowing for any middle ground. However, this polarity is not an *inherent* characteristic of concepts; conceptual space supports bottom-up intuition and top-down visualization, neither of which is a binary operation.

The interpretation of sensation, on the other hand, forces concepts to be discrete and to occur serially.[65] As a result, people who persistently structure their experience using symbols are

---

[64] The sensation that is available to collect into concepts is determined by both sensory (or bottom-up) activation and conceptual (or top-down) inhibition.

[65] Both zeroth-order and higher-order concepts can operate in parallel with one another after they have been learned experientially, since both can be activated bottom-up, but when activated top-down by symbols, they are limited to serial operation.

particularly prone to black-and-white thinking, since the effect of symbolic thought is to exclude experience that does not fit the given conceptual model.[66] It is therefore useful to differentiate these two modes of conceptual activation, one which is bottom-up, subsymbolic, and commonly associated with zeroth-order concepts, and one which is top-down, symbolic, and more often associated with higher-order concepts. The distinction between them is somewhat blurred because these systems overlap in practice.

3.6.3.3 Conceptual Dimensions
Conceptual dimensions form a space that can be either continuous or discrete.

Concepts are wholes of sensation. They are similar to transparent containers, for which sensation provides the content. As containers, their nature depends on their content. In particular, if continuous parts are collected, the whole forms a continuous space, while if discrete parts are collected, the whole forms a discrete space. In both cases, the collection of parts results in a whole of larger size, and therefore the effect of creating composite concepts is to increase conceptual granularity.

In addition to creating wholes, concepts composed of symbols create nominal dimensions, and therefore nominal identity. Implications of this fact are discussed further in section *Symbolic Space* (p. 91).

---

[66] Because symbolic thought causes an inhibition of what is unattended, the top-down influence of a single concept can make us perceive (and thereby know) less. For example, a hungry mind categorizes experiences only as food or not-food, while other distinctions become invisible. This is contrary to how concepts are implicitly believed to work, since the occurrence of a concept is often taken as an indication of knowing *more* (see section *Attention*, p. 140).

The Number of Conceptual Dimensions
The number of conceptual dimensions is unlimited.

The dimensionality of a single concept depends in part on its *order*. The dimensionality of a zeroth-order concept is equal to the dimensionality of its composite sensation, as creating a conceptual whole does not inherently increase or decrease dimensionality.[67]

The dimensionality of a higher-order concept, however, can be regarded as one more than the dimensionality of its constituent symbols. This is because symbols are discrete atoms; therefore, concepts composed of symbols are 1-D unordered collections. Those concepts can also be interpreted as having a dimensionality that is one greater than the dimensionality of what their constituent symbols represent. In this way, the dimensionality of referential space is extended by creating a nominal dimension that ranges over its references, as illustrated in section *Symbolic Dimensions* (p. 92).

The Nature of Conceptual Dimensions
Conceptual dimensions are continuous or discrete in virtue of their contents.

As with the number of dimensions, the nature of conceptual dimensions also depends on the order of the concepts in question. Concrete zeroth-order concepts are wholes of sensation that exist in the same mereological space as their parts. Therefore, they are effectively (if not entirely) continuous, since the granularity of sensation is extremely fine. They are also concrete, just as sensation is concrete. For example, if one learns the zeroth-order concept "small dog"$_\varphi$ in virtue of experience with several small dogs (dog_1, dog_2, dog_3, ...), that concept exists as a concrete conceptual union of dog experiences, with numerous

---

[67] A counterexample to this generality happens in the visual pathway, where the dimensionality of the representation increases (see section *Sensory Dimensions*, p. 72).

contextual associations such as that small dogs bark at a high pitch.

On the other hand, when a higher-order concept is learned by logically combining the concepts *small$_\varphi$* and *dog$_\varphi$*, no such contextual associations are learned. Rather, the intersection of two concepts occurs when the two abstract ideas small$_\varphi$ and dog$_\varphi$ are combined (since what is intended is clearly not the union of all small things and all dog things). In doing so, higher-order concepts become abstract. For further discussion of this process, see section <u>Higher-Order Concepts</u> (p. 96).

Chapter 7
Epistemic Relations

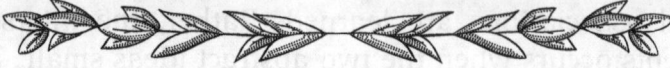

Six epistemic relations are defined between the objective, sensory, and conceptual spaces.

This chapter looks at the six relations between the three epistemic universes of the basic model. These six relations may be summarized as follows with respect to the objective (**O**), sensory (**N**), and conceptual (**C**) spaces, and where symbolic space (**V**, a subspace of sensory space) is denoted explicitly:

- **Sensation (Θ):** Sensation is a *causal* function. It changes **N** as a result of **O**.

- **Action (Δ):** Action is a *causal* function. It changes **O** as a result of **C**.

- **Conceptualization (Φ):** Conceptualization is the *whole* function. It creates increasingly conceptual wholes as one moves from **N** to **C**.

- **Visualization (Ψ):** Visualization is the *part* function. It creates increasingly sensory parts as one moves from **C** to **N**.

- **Interpretation (Ω):** Interpretation is the *referent* function. It activates referents in **C** in virtue of symbolic references in **V**.

- **Symbolization (Ξ):** Symbolization is the *reference* function. It activates symbolic references in **V** in virtue of referents in **C**.

3.7.1 Sensation

Sensation affects sensory space as a result of changes in objective space.

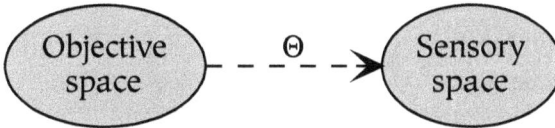

Figure 3.7.1: Sensation (Θ) is the dual of action.

There are at least two important points to note about sensation, which creates sensations in sensory space from objects in objective space.

The first is that it creates a mass of *sensation*, rather than individuated sensations. Sensation is individuated, combined, and divided by subsequent conceptualization and visualization; new sensation is not produced in this process. In other words, the entire content of our experience of the world is provided via sensation (e.g., sensation includes things like feelings and emotions).

The second is that sensation is the dual of action. Just as action causes effects in the world, sensation causes effects in us. However, the English grammar describing both events implies that the person is the agent, since the person both senses and acts. This asymmetry is unfortunate, since sensation is caused by the action of the external object (i.e., it is similar to saying that a baseball *senses* the bat that hits it, when in fact it doesn't have much of a choice in the matter).

3.7.2 **Action**

Action affects objective space as a result of changes in conceptual space.

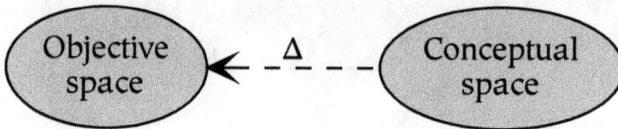

Figure 3.7.2: Action (Δ) is the dual of sensation.

Action changes the physical world according to the conceptual intent of an individual, through acts such as walking or the creation of sound waves.[68] When the actions are sounds such as spoken words, action may also convey interpersonal symbolic content.[69]

3.7.3 **Conceptualization**

Conceptualization creates conceptual wholes from sensory parts.

The creation of concepts entails the bottom-up collection of sensation and concepts into a single whole. Concepts can also be

---

[68] Although action is depicted here as originating from conceptual space for simplicity, it is probably better represented as a mapping from subjective space to objective space.

[69] Although the basic model treats the physical universe as the source of everything, it is also a destination. Similarly, just as our sensation is caused by the world, the world is caused by our actions. Given the coexistence of these universes, perhaps the determination of which universe existed first is merely the result of one's point of view. For example, perhaps the scientific tradition that maintains that the physical universe existed before there was anything to perceive it, and the spiritual and idealist traditions that maintain that the creation of the universe required an act of perception, are compatible and complimentary points of view.

composed of symbols, in which case they are called higher-order concepts. Conceptualization can generally operate in parallel, although emotional attachment and top-down symbolic activation may enforce serial operation.

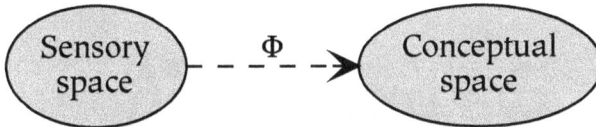

Figure 3.7.3: Conceptualization (Φ) is the dual of visualization.

3.7.4 Visualization

Visualization creates sensory parts from conceptual wholes.

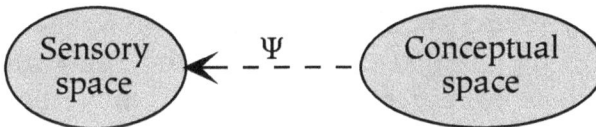

Figure 3.7.4: Visualization (Ψ) is the dual of conceptualization.

Visualization entails the top-down projection of concepts to sensory space. It may be seen as a transformation of concepts back into sense data, or at least a transformation of percepts from a higher to a lower epistemic level. It therefore operates in a direction opposite to conceptualization.

Visualization is not necessarily visual, although visual imagery is often used to describe this process (as in the word *imagination*). Since partial visualization makes conceptual parts out of larger conceptual wholes, but does not necessarily create "raw" sensation, it is similar to understanding.[70] Visualization is capable of turning multiple concepts into a single concrete unit, which may be the mechanism behind the psychological process of chunking.[71]

3.7.5 Interpretation

Interpretation activates concepts in conceptual space from symbols in symbolic space.

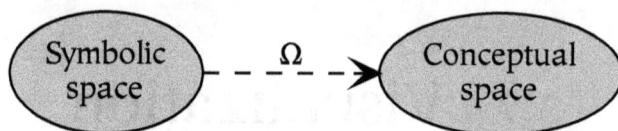

Figure 3.7.5: Interpretation (Ω) is the dual of symbolization.

Interpretation is an act of dereferencing that creates meaning from a sensory reference. These perceptual references are known as symbols. In the context of cognition, they may also be called *cognitive symbols* to differentiate them from verbal or written symbols.

Interpretation entails the activation of a concept based on its name. In other words, symbols are symbolizations of their corresponding concepts, and concepts are interpretations of their corresponding symbols. Interpretation is therefore similar to conceptualization, but unlike conceptualization, the interpretation of a sensation is not a mereological whole of that sensation.

---

[70] Understanding entails knowing both the parts and wholes of an object, while visualization pertains only to rendering parts.

[71] This is supported by experimental evidence from various chunking strategies, which often utilize concrete mnemonic cues such as walking along a path.

3.7.6 Symbolization

*Symbolization creates symbols in symbolic space
from concepts in conceptual space.*

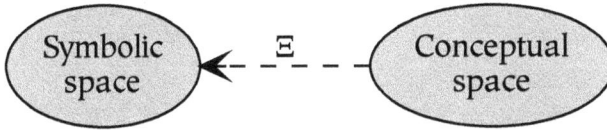

Figure 3.7.6: Symbolization (Ξ) is the dual of interpretation.

Symbolization is an act of naming that takes place between a sensation (or the reference) and a concept (or the referent). The sensation becomes the name or *symbol* for that concept, and thus forms the basis for symbolic thought. For example, the vocalized word earth$_\xi$ is the name for the concept earth$_\varphi$.[72]

Symbolization is the dual of interpretation. It resembles visualization in that it produces sensation (i.e., the symbol) from a corresponding concept, but it is different in that the sensation it creates is not a mereological part of that concept. It is perhaps better understood as an internalized shorthand for an *action* followed by the *sensation* resulting from that act (e.g., such as occurs in the process of subvocalization and hearing when learning words).

---

[72] Children often learn words by going through a subvocalization process of internalizing words. To the extent that symbols are no longer associated with auditory sensation, symbolic space becomes a separate "mental sense".

Chapter 8
Recursion

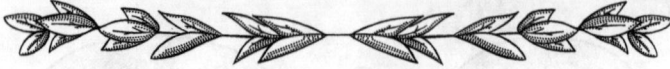

*The interaction of subjective spaces and their relations
creates higher-order cognition and symbolic spaces.*

Symbols are references to concepts that form *symbolic space*.
Symbols are specialized types of sensation: for example, the word
$wind_\xi$ is a part of our sensory space that becomes a symbol for
the concept $wind_\varphi$. The combination of concepts that are
composed of sensation and symbols that refer to concepts
establishes the basis for a referential recursion between sensory
and conceptual spaces that is illustrated in Figure 3.8a.

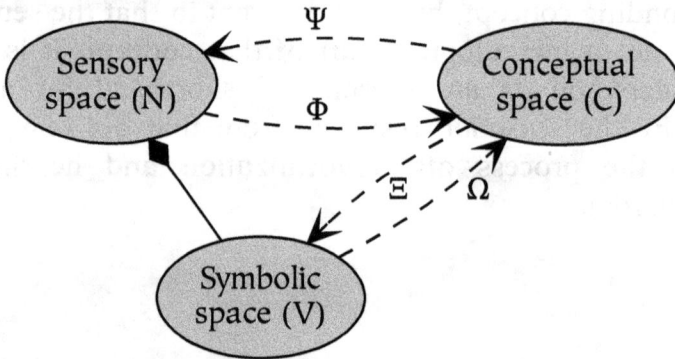

**Figure 3.8a: Symbolic space is the part of sensory space
that references conceptual space.**

Figure 3.8b depicts an unrolled version of this sensory/
conceptual recursion. Each node's label is annotated with a
superscript indicating the <u>conceptual order</u>, and to the right of
each node is a number that indicates the epistemic level.

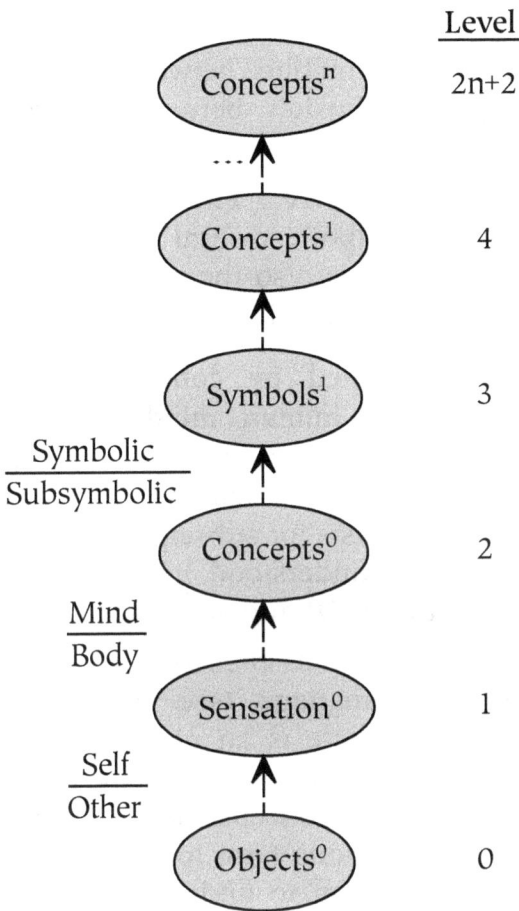

Figure 3.8b: Epistemic level indicates distance from ground.

The left side of Figure 3.8b shows the approximate locations of three popular epistemic divisions, each of which traditionally corresponds to a mereological distinction rather than a purely referential distinction:

◆ **Self/Other**: The self/other distinction epistemically corresponds most closely to the distinction between sensations and objects.

♦ **Body/Mind**: The distinction between body and mind is approximately the division between nonconceptual and conceptual.

♦ **Subsymbolic/Symbolic**: The distinction between subsymbolic and symbolic mental content is made at the level of symbols. This is also the division between abstract universals and concrete particulars.

The loop that is formed by conceptualization (Φ) and symbolization (Ξ) allows human minds to create symbolic hierarchies. This loop enables recursive composition, whereby conceptual wholes are represented by symbols, and those symbols in turn form the basis for subsequent conceptual wholes. These hierarchies can be understood by reversing this process, which entails interpretation (Ω) and visualization (Ψ).

In linguistics, the hierarchies thus constructed correspond to the deep structure of language (see [Chomsky, 1995]). In mathematical set theory, there is an analogous structure called the Zermelo or von Neumann Hierarchy. Cognitively, the construction of higher-order concepts out of previously existing concepts is leveraged both long-term to define words as higher-order concepts and short-term to understand sentences that are dynamically-constructed.

The depth of these hierarchies can be quantified using the notion of *epistemic level*. Epistemic level is a measure of the number of transitions (or arrows) that must be traversed to reach ground, which has an epistemic level of zero by definition. Epistemic level therefore increases every time things are sensed, conceptualized, or symbolized, and decreases with every act, visualization, or interpretation.

3.8.1 Symbolic Space
Symbolic space is the space of symbols,
or sensations that reference concepts.

Symbolic space is the subspace of sensation whose parts are interpreted symbolically. Therefore, symbolic space is literally a *mental sense*, which is distinct from the conceptual understanding to which it corresponds.[73]

Cognitive symbols (or simply symbols) are meaningful in terms of both their conceptual content and their relation to other symbols. The relation of symbols to one another is determined by their common wholes, and is explored further in section *Language* (p. 106).

3.8.1.1 The Conceptual/Symbolic Dichotomy
Although symbols are parts in mereological space,
they are references in referential space.

Symbols may be experienced either non-referentially as sensation or in virtue of their referential content. The results of directly conceptualizing that symbol as opposed to interpreting that symbol are dramatically different. Cognitively, this decision is somewhat of a forced choice, because the conceptualization of a symbol and the interpretation of that symbol tend to destructively interfere with one another.[74]

---

[73] Although the term "symbol" often corresponds in other contexts to both internal thoughts and external written or spoken words, symbolic space consists exclusively of *cognitive* symbols.

[74] This interference is described in a number of sources such as [Baddeley, 2001]. The *necessity* of this destructive interference is an important question, since it would be advantageous to have access to non-degraded semantic *and* episodic content.

As an example of this interference, consider perceiving symbols without additionally interpreting them, as happens when listening to speakers of an unfamiliar language. Although there is awareness of various auditory characteristics of the words such as the pitch, volume, and timbre, the meaning of the words is not understood. In contrast, interpretation of the words when listening to a familiar language often causes the sensory detail of the sound of those words to be lost.[75]

3.8.1.2 Symbolic Parts
The parts of symbolic space are called symbols.

An essential characteristic of symbols is that they must activate (or re-present) the same concepts as does perceiving the physical object which they designate. However, unlike the sensations that trigger that concept, they are not required to resemble that object at a sensory level.

Because symbolic understanding destructively interferes with the bottom-up perception of environmental stimuli, symbols must inhibit those competing stimuli in order to activate their intended meaning. This process of preventing irrelevant bottom-up activation from interfering also prevents any other symbols from being simultaneously active. As a result, symbols are understood serially rather than in parallel.

3.8.1.3 Symbolic Dimensions
Because symbols are discrete references, their collection into wholes forms a discrete space.

Symbolic space is composed of discrete (symbolic) references. In other words, since references are not divisible in a meaningful

---

[75] The trade-off between sensation and conceptualization applies not just to other people's speech, but to one's own thought. In other words, it is possible to either sense or conceptualize one's own thought process, depending on the epistemic level to which one pays attention.

way, symbols correspond to discrete atoms within symbolic space. As such, they may be treated as geometric points, although they have unit extent rather than zero extent.[76] An example atom is depicted in Figure 3.8.1a, where it is assumed that the atom is not mereologically divisible (despite its apparent volume).

Figure 3.8.1a: An atom (zero discrete dimensions).

Symbolic dimensions, or the dimensions formed by collecting symbols within a referential space, can be synthesized by combining these referential atoms. For example, a reference can be combined with references to its left and right, thereby forming a line of references. This is depicted in Figure 3.8.1b, where an atom iterated in an arbitrary direction results in a line.[77]

Figure 3.8.1b: A line (one discrete dimension).

This process can be repeated: a line creates a plane when iterated in a direction orthogonal to its length, as shown in Figure 3.8.1c. Similarly, many planes collected along an orthogonal dimension form a 3-D cube, as in Figure 3.8.1d.

---

[76] The dimensionality of atoms in this section refers to the dimensionality along which they are differentiable. Thus an atom, even if it exists as a non-empty volume within a high-dimensional space, does not have any discrete dimensionality because it is not differentiable along any dimension.

[77] A line constructed in this way is not entirely equivalent to a mathematical line, since it begins with a discrete atom instead of a point: therefore, this process increases the dimensionality of a discrete space, but not a continuous space.

Figure 3.8.1c: A plane (two discrete dimensions).

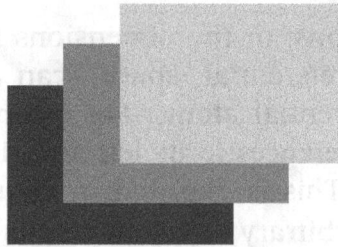

Figure 3.8.1d: A cube (three discrete dimensions).

In the physical universe, the fourth dimension is called time (at least by physicists).[78] As with the previous dimensions, a novel dimension is created by iterating a lower-dimensional object along a new axis that is orthogonal to the existing ones, as in Figure 3.8.1e.

The depiction of a 5-D object is a particularly interesting example of how each successive dimension is produced, because few people have explicitly extended their conceptualization (or visualization) of dimensionality that far.[79] Implicitly, however,

---

[78] Time is said to move in only one direction, so it seems different from the other spatial dimensions, though its apparent unidirectionality is a result of using entropy to measure its direction.

[79] The most obvious options for introducing a fifth dimension are either adding a dimension after the temporal or adding a new dimension in the penultimate position (i.e., preserving time as the last coordinate). The second option creates objects such as the Necker Cube, which has four spatial dimensions and no temporal dimensions.

the fifth dimension is used frequently as the measure of possibility. The fifth dimension is not a difficult concept to grasp when understood in this way, although it is not explicitly treated as a spatial dimension.

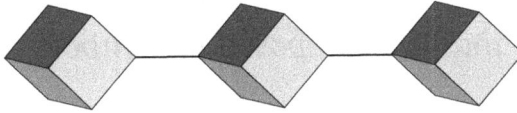

Figure 3.8.1e: A timeline (four discrete dimensions).

To conceptualize the five-dimensional world, it is helpful to imagine another earth that is similar to ours, which exists at the same place and time (or at the same spatial and temporal coordinates), but which occupies a different fifth dimensional coordinate. In philosophical terms, it is a possible world instead of the actual one. Visually, since four dimensions are represented by a world-line, the fifth dimension can be represented by multiple world-lines, as shown in Figure 3.8.1f.

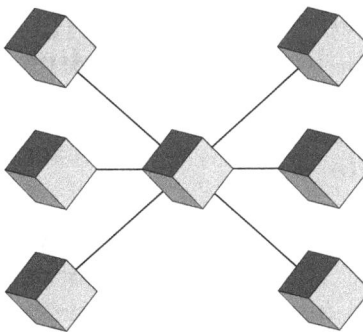

Figure 3.8.1f: Multiple timelines (five discrete dimensions).

Because the fifth dimension enables the discussion of possible worlds, it is referred to as the dimension of modality. Support for the hypothesis that the world is at least 5-D, or that objects exist in multiple possible states at once, is given by experiments in physics such as the double-slit experiment.

3.8.2 Higher-Order Concepts

Higher-order concepts are concepts that are composed of symbols.

Table 3.8.2a: Two Kinds of Concepts.

Zeroth-Order Concepts	Higher-Order Concepts
Can be contiguous or discontiguous	Are necessarily discontiguous
Do not support generalization	Support generalization
Are concrete	Are abstract
Support unitization	Do not support unitization
Do not create an equivalence class	Create an equivalence class
Have fixed dimensionality	Have varying dimensionality
Are composed of percepts	Are composed of percepts that are symbols

Concepts may be either concrete or abstract. Concrete or zeroth-order concepts are conceptual wholes that are constituted by sensation or by other concrete concepts directly. Abstract or higher-order concepts are wholes of symbolic references, and as such, their order is one more than their constituent concepts. For example, if tree$_\varphi$ is defined as the abstract conceptual whole composed of pine$_\xi$ and maple$_\xi$, and both pine$_\xi$ and maple$_\xi$ are symbols standing for first-order concepts, then the nominal dimension used to contain these two symbols makes tree$_\varphi$ a second-order concept.

The ubiquity of concepts in different disciplines has led to an abundance of terminology. For example, the following terms are at least approximately synonymous with concepts: wholes, generalizations, unitizations, categories, abstractions, generalities, sets, classes, and equivalence classes. Since the meaning of these terms is imprecise given their somewhat differing use in multiple contexts, Table 3.8.2a clarifies how some of those terms are used here. Several of these terms require further comment, especially with respect to the critical distinction between concrete and abstract concepts:

Contiguity: Higher-order concepts are formed by collecting category members; therefore, they are conceptually granular or chunky. They also tend to represent objects that are discontiguous, since contiguous objects can be represented with zeroth-order concepts.[80]

Unitization: Unitization refers to the process of making successive wholes (or unions of parts) without increasing the order of the concept. It is thus the conceptual operation that corresponds to creating meronomies from concrete parts. For example, the concepts head$_\varphi$, torso$_\varphi$, arms$_\varphi$, and legs$_\varphi$ may constitute the first-order concept of a body$_\varphi$ without requiring any intermediary symbols. Although it is possible to form a meronomy of abstract parts, this is generally not intended (this is explored further in the next section, *Cognitive Taxonomies*, p. 102).

To understand the difference between unitizations and generalizations, imagine an apple and an orange. The unitization of these two (i.e., their zeroth-order concept) is the *union* of all sensations of the apple and the orange; it is a concrete,

---

[80] It may be that zeroth-order concepts are *necessarily* contiguous. In either case, discontiguous concepts are almost certainly more difficult to form due to cognitive constraints, since they go against the principles of Gestalt concept formation.

mereological fusion. On the other hand, the abstract generalization of apple and orange concepts is the *intersection* of their corresponding <u>ideas</u>, or all parts and wholes of apples and oranges.

Abstraction or **generalization**: Abstraction entails the formation of a categorical *prototype*, whose properties are common to the constituent concepts of that category.[81] As mentioned previously, when zeroth-order concepts are formed, they are wholes of their composite sensation. Therefore, they are concrete, just as that sensation is concrete. However, when higher-order concepts are understood, the necessary visualization of their constituent symbols makes them abstract.

Symbols become abstract when an intersection of their conceptual content is formed to isolate specific properties. For example, the property *green*$_\varphi$ may be isolated from green trees and green moss by forming the intersection of the constituent properties of those objects. Similarly, the meaning of the higher-order concept "pet dogs"$_\varphi$ involves the intersection of properties belonging to pet$_\varphi$ and dog$_\varphi$ ideas, which makes sense even to a person who knows what pets and dogs are, but who has never physically encountered a pet dog.

The reason that higher-order concepts form intersections is that symbols are visualized by negating the *opposite* of their referent concepts, where the opposite means all concepts which are not parts or wholes of the given concept. When two symbols are combined in this top-down manner, the resulting concept exists as the intersection of the two ideas. This process makes a concept abstract if the intersection *lacks any location*, which happens when the constituent concepts have disjoint spatial locations.[82]

---

[81] Generalizations may be understood as propositions, or functions that produce a truth value as a result. For example, the propositional function *isaTree(x)* indicates the presence of a tree.

[82] The dimensionality of an abstract concept or property is *less than* the dimensionality of its constituent concepts, and determined by the degree to

However, it is not true that the visualization of concepts is always abstract. Take as examples the zeroth-order concepts chair$_{\varphi 1}$ and chair$_{\varphi 2}$, which are composed of the union or unitization of the sensations derived from two chairs, chair$_1$ and chair$_2$. There may be a composite zeroth-order concept, chair$_{\varphi 3}$, that exists as the conceptual unitization of those two chair concepts. Understanding chair$_{\varphi 3}$ entails only visualization of that union, rather than forming the intersection of two interpreted symbols. Therefore, the resulting concept remains concrete, unlike the higher-order concept that is formed out of the two symbols chair$_{\xi 1}$ and chair$_{\xi 2}$. To reiterate, although the physical intersection of two distinct concrete entities is necessarily empty, the intersection of the chair$_{\varphi 1}$ and chair$_{\varphi 2}$ ideas is not necessarily empty because they share a number of abstract wholes or properties (such as being places to sit).[83]

The combination of these examples means that concepts can be defined both in an absolute sense (via zeroth-order, concrete sensation) and in a relative sense (via higher-order, abstract concepts), which corresponds to the fact that things in the world are known by both experience and definition.[84] In practice, since few concepts exist purely in a zeroth-order or higher-order way, it is impossible to assign them a unique order.

---

which the constituent concepts of a higher-order concept overlap. In this way, abstractness/concreteness can be viewed as a continuum that increases with dimensionality.

[83] In other words, since the *ideas* corresponding to the two chair symbols entail the activation of all parts and wholes of those chair concepts, the intersection of those two symbols is not empty to the extent that they have common parts and wholes.

[84] In psychological terms, categories are defined using both exemplar theory and prototype theory.

3.8.2.1 Cognitive Meronomies
Knowing entails structural relations between concepts.

To know the relations between objects in the world entails structuring the references to those objects in a particular manner. In order to examine the different ways in which this knowledge might be structured, imagine a world in which there is a cat named "Felix", who has a paw (called "Felix's paw"). Given a diagram of these conceptual entities, how can one represent that *cats have paws*? In other words, what is the structure of conceptual space such that its referential structure is isomorphic to the structure in the world between cats and paws?

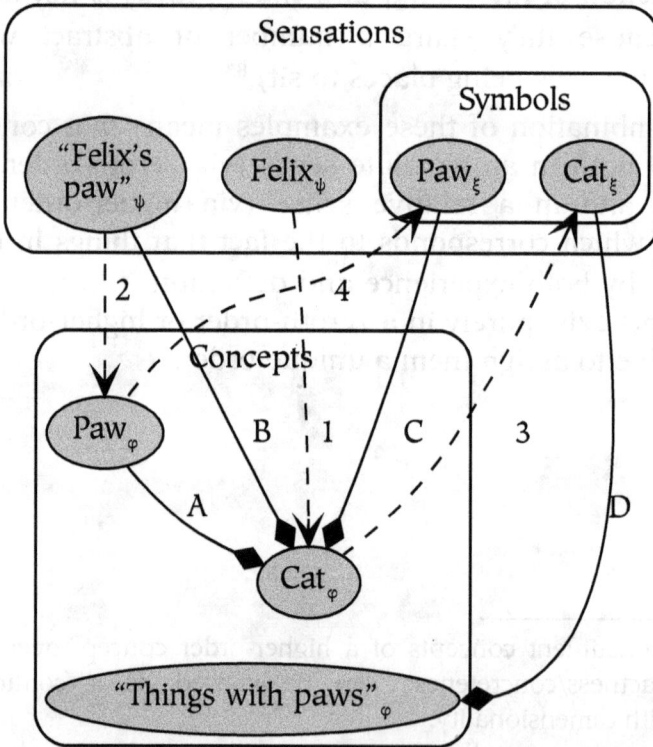

Figure 3.8.2b: Arrows A–D illustrate several ways of knowing that "cats have paws".

The cognitive structure in which we hope to represent this information is shown in Figure 3.8.2b, where the relations shown by dashed arrows indicate that:

1. $cat_\varphi = \Phi(Felix_\psi)$: $Felix_\psi$ is a cat_φ.
2. $paw_\varphi = \Phi(\text{"Felix's paw"}_\psi)$: "Felix's paw"$_\psi$ is a paw_φ.
3. $cat_\xi = \Xi(cat_\varphi)$: the name of the concept cat_φ is cat_ξ.
4. $paw_\xi = \Xi(paw_\varphi)$: the name of the concept paw_φ is paw_ξ.

There are at least several implementation options, which correspond to the solid edges in the diagram:

A. **cat_φ is a whole of paw_φ**: This option seems like the most obvious answer. Together with relation (1), it creates concepts that are composed of both sensory and conceptual content. It is a relation between concrete entities, however, so it does not capture the universality of "cats have paws".

B. **cat_φ is a whole of "Felix's paw"$_\psi$**: This option creates a concept cat_φ that is composed only of sensations (i.e., $Felix_\psi$ and "Felix's paw"$_\psi$).

C. **cat_φ is a whole of paw_ξ**: The drawback of this option is that the concept cat_φ becomes constituted by both sensation (e.g., $Felix_\psi$) and symbols (e.g., paw_ξ), which makes it an uncomfortable amalgamation of different epistemic levels.[85]

D. **"Things with paws"$_\varphi$ is a whole of cat_ξ**: This option is slightly redundant because it involves a usage of paws which is not connected to the concept of paw_φ.

E. **(not depicted)**: In order to know if cats have paws, the existing concrete concepts can be visualized in sensory

---

[85] This is obviously a bit weird, but that doesn't rule it out, because so are humans. Intuitively, however, a conceptual mixture of different referential levels does not seem correct. For more astute observations on this issue, see [Lewis, 1991].

space, where the parthood relationship can be determined by inspection.

While option (E) may be necessary for visualization or intuition, it is not a solution to the issue of how to store knowledge between abstract concepts. The cleanest solution allows this relation to be modeled in two different ways, which express slightly different things. Options (A) and (B) express the relation "concrete cats have concrete paws" as a concrete meronomy, and option (D) expresses the relation "abstract cats have abstract paws" as an abstract taxonomy. One notable aspect of this pair of solutions is that there is no immediate connection between the concrete concept paw_φ and the abstract property "things with paws"$_\varphi$ (this is not a very elegant finding architecturally, although it may not be incorrect from a cognitive perspective). Another notable aspect is that "things with paws"$_\varphi$ is typically modeled in prototype theory as a property, although in the basic model it is modeled as a symbolic (abstract) whole.

3.8.2.2 Cognitive Taxonomies

Higher-order concepts are composed of symbols that reference concepts, rather than composing concepts directly.

In order to explore how higher-order concepts such as "things with paws"$_\varphi$ are constructed, Figure 3.8.2c shows several relations and entities in the objective, sensory, and conceptual spaces. Objective space is depicted at the top level, which causes the sensations a_ψ, $b_{\psi 1}$, and $b_{\psi 2}$ in sensory space.[86] These sensations are conceptualized as a_φ and b_φ in conceptual space. Finally, these concepts are united in a higher-order concept, c_φ.

---

[86] In this diagram, the objective universe is not depicted as divided into a dog and a cat, which would imply that they exist as natural kinds. That said, objects are labelled as individual entities elsewhere in this book as a matter of convenience.

Figure 3.8.2c can be made more concrete by visualizing it as the description of a world that consists of one dog and one cat. Dog and cat concepts (a_φ and b_φ) are formed by sensing the dog once ($a_{\psi1}$) and the cat twice ($b_{\psi1}$, $b_{\psi2}$). The dog and the cat are both kinds of the abstract type *animal* (c_φ).

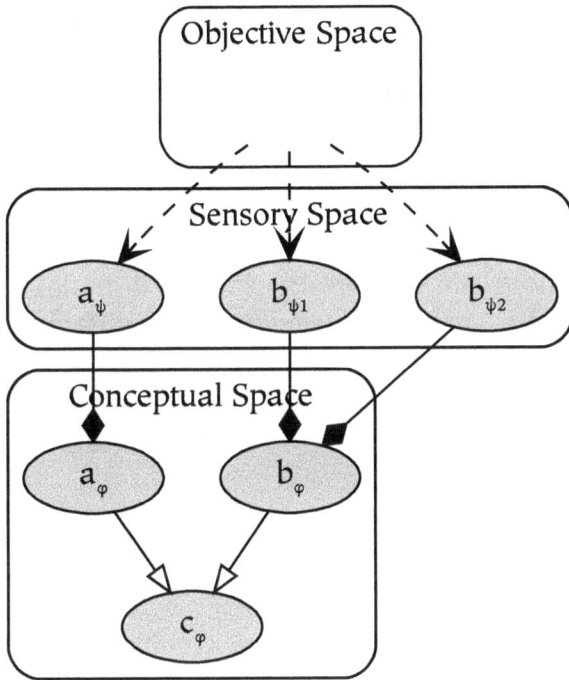

Figure 3.8.2c: The structure of a higher-order concept (c_φ).

Although this diagram may accurately represent the structure of knowing, the generalization relation that is indicated by empty-triangle arrowheads that point towards c_φ is a shorthand that has not been defined using the relations that exist in the basic model. Therefore, the rest of this section explores how the generalization relation can be implemented using wholes (conceptualization), parts (visualization), referents (interpretation), and references (symbolization).

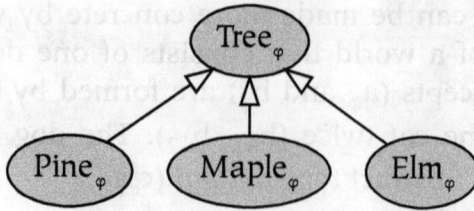

**Figure 3.8.2d: A taxonomy using the undefined
generalization relation:
Tree$_\varphi$ = generalization(Pine$_\varphi$, Maple$_\varphi$, Elm$_\varphi$).**

Figure 3.8.2d depicts an abstract taxonomy. The most obvious choice for implementing this structure without the generalization relation uses the operation of *whole* to create a meronomy, although that does not capture the intended meaning because the leaf nodes are abstract. In other words, an abstract tree does not have abstract pines and maples as parts; rather, pines and maples are kinds of trees. Therefore, meronomies such as the one in Figure 3.8.2e are generally inaccurate, as discussed in section <u>Meronomies</u> (p. 39).

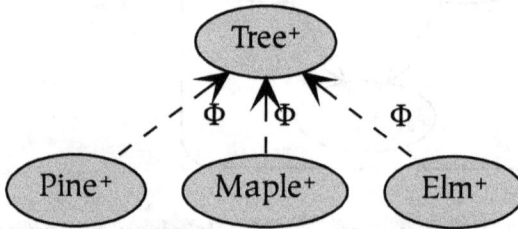

**Figure 3.8.2e: An invalid conceptual meronomy with
abstract conceptual elements
Tree$_\varphi$ = whole(Pine$_\varphi$, Maple$_\varphi$, Elm$_\varphi$)**

Valid methods for implementing the taxonomy are illustrated in Figures 3.8.2f and 3.8.2g, each of which has different cognitive consequences. The first method is depicted in Figure 3.8.2f, and entails turning the conceptual wholes back into sense data and then collecting that sense data into a new conceptual whole.

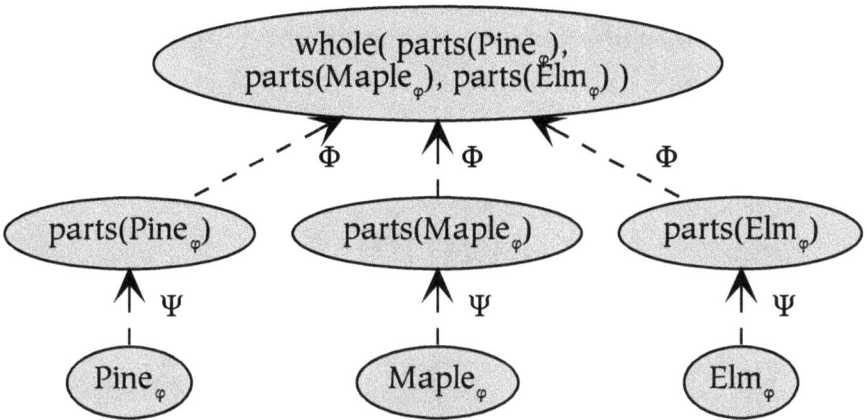

Figure 3.8.2f: A sensory meronomy
$Tree_\varphi = whole(Pine_\psi, Maple_\psi, Elm_\psi)$

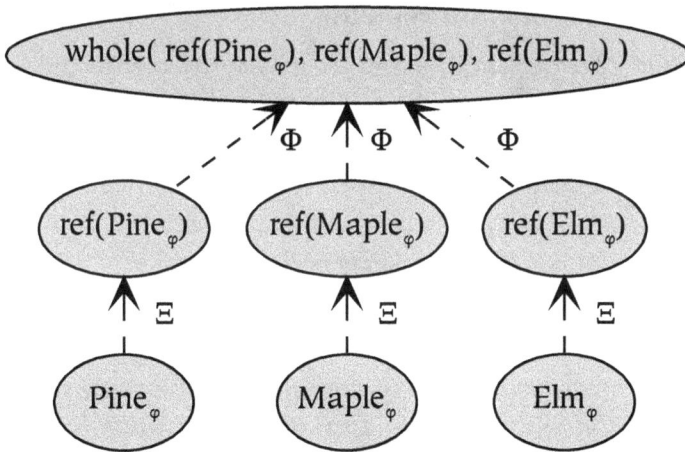

Figure 3.8.2g: A symbolic meronomy
$Tree_\varphi = whole(Pine_\xi, Maple_\xi, Elm_\xi)$

The second method is depicted in Figure 3.8.2g, and entails creating symbolic references to the wholes and then collecting those symbols into a new, higher-order conceptual whole. The difference between these two structures is that the first one does not increase the <u>conceptual order</u> of the concept tree$_\varphi$. In other words, the tree$_\varphi$ of the sensory meronomy is of the same order as its constituents, while the tree$_\varphi$ of the symbolic meronomy is one order higher than its constituents as a result of creating symbolic references to them.

3.8.3 Language

Languages are dynamic systems for expressing and understanding conceptual space.

Symbolic space is a discrete space that is composed of symbols and which represents conceptual space. In order to express that symbolic space intersubjectively, humans use words and language. Since abstract parts of speech require higher-order concepts, language involving syntactically complex sentences is generally possible only for humans

Language can be understood as a way to create meaning from conceptual structures, which are in turn derived from a series of abstract parts of speech.[87] The next three sections briefly explore three aspects of language: semantics, syntax, and sentences.

3.8.3.1 Semantics

Semantics is the study of symbolic meaning.

Concepts have two kinds of semantics, one with respect to the sensory and conceptual parts that they compose, and one with respect to the conceptual wholes of which they form a part. These two kinds of semantics form the absolute and relative meaning of those concepts. Mathematically, they are analogous to the intension and extension of a set.

---

[87] The main goal of this section is to show how the basic model of cognition interfaces with the study of syntax and semantics. Since these subjects are extremely complicated, this presentation necessarily omits numerous details.

To learn an object as a zeroth-order concept requires emotional motivation and direct experiences with that object. When such experiences happen a sufficient number of times, a conceptual whole is formed that consists of concepts corresponding to the parts of that object, and which in turn forms a part of the larger conceptual contexts in which that object appears. Thus, the semantics of zeroth-order concepts depends on the concrete parts and wholes of the corresponding object, or its mereological context.

To learn what an object is as a higher-order concept requires knowing its abstract (symbolic) parts and wholes. For example, the meaning of the abstract concept $tree_\varphi$ derives from pines and maples being kinds of trees, and trees in turn being kinds of plants. Further, the meaning of the concept $tree_\varphi$ also derives from things it is not; for example, the digram in Figure 3.8.3a illustrates that trees are plants that are not house plants.[88]

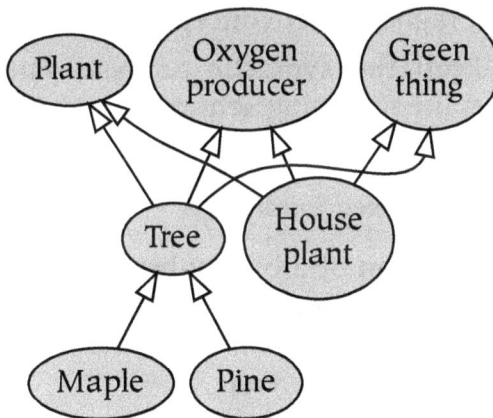

Figure 3.8.3a: Trees, presented in an abstract taxonomic context.

Figure 3.8.3a may not be a typical model of the cognition of city dwellers, in that it depicts $tree_\varphi$ as a concept that is a

---

[88] While this epistemological context is important for all symbols of which one knows the definition, it is essential to understand objects with which one does not have direct experience.

composite of other higher-order concepts. For people not living in nature, tree$_\varphi$ is more likely a <u>basic category</u> that is learned without symbolically differentiating the different types of trees.[89]

3.8.3.2 Syntax
Syntax is the study of symbolic combination.

One of the most interesting features of syntax is that it allows a collection of preexisting symbols to produce a novel semantic result. As a result, while the concept ice$_\varphi$ is known on a concrete basis to residents of Canada, it may be known only on an abstract basis to residents of a hot country with no refrigeration (i.e., where there is no ice). In other words, residents of that hot country know ice$_\varphi$ only by its definition: solid, cold water.[90] This process of using syntax to recombine known concepts is used both dynamically to understand language, and as the underlying structure to create higher-order concepts.

In order to keep the syntactic analysis fairly simple, this section focuses on the following sentence (and ignores its definite article, "the"):[91]

The green frog croaked loudly.

Under the assumption of a binary-branching syntax with verb phrases (VP), noun phrases (NP), adjectives (ADJ), adverbs (ADV), nouns (N), and verbs (V), the syntactic production rules for this sentence may be written as:

---

[89] The categories at the epistemic level where concepts change from concrete to abstract are known in cognitive science as *basic level categories*.

[90] Equivalently, *ice* can be understood as everything after removing all things that are not solid, not cold, and not watery.

[91] Definite articles are modifiers which reduce the abstraction of the object to which they are applied. For more information, see [http://theWholePart.com/essays].

$$S \rightarrow VP\ (NP)$$
$$NP \rightarrow ADJ\ (N)$$
$$VP \rightarrow ADV\ (V)$$

These rules are sufficient to create the deep structure of the sentence, but they are not sufficiently detailed to show how various parts of speech relate to concepts. To begin, the sentence is analyzed into the following parts of speech:

$green_{ADJ}$, $frog_N$, $croaked_V$, $loudly_{ADV}$

Applying the syntactic rules given above to these parts of speech results in the syntax tree depicted in Figure 3.8.3b. Since each of these parts of speech correspond to cognitive symbols, the parsed sentence may also be represented as:

$loudly_\xi(\ croaked_\xi\ )\ (\ green_\xi(\ frog_\xi\ )\ )$

As the sentence is constructed, the symbols of the sentence are visualized one after the other. Since the noun "frog" is the deepest part of the structure, it is the first concept to be visualized and understood.

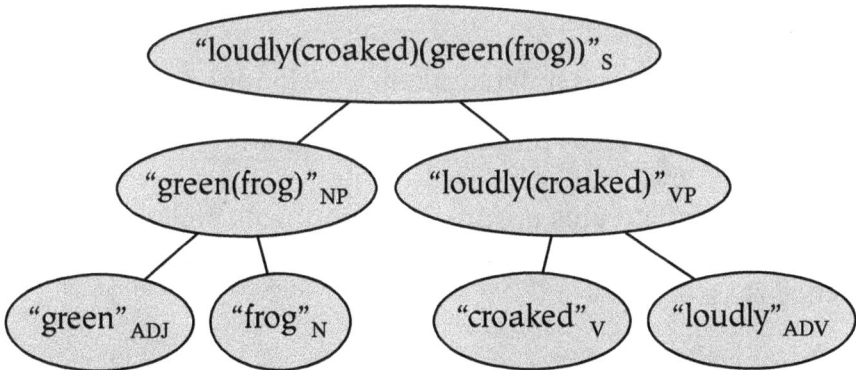

Figure 3.8.3b: The deep structure of the phrase "green frog croaked loudly".

This syntactic process can be modeled with more precision by augmenting the intuitive understanding of nouns and verbs with a more formal notion that includes their dimensionality. In particular, the recombination of abstract parts of speech such as nouns (which lack any temporal aspect) and verbs (which lack any spatial aspect) results in sentences that can be visualized in a concrete, high-dimensional space. In this example, if the dimensionality of the entire sentence is n, then the dimensionality of frog is $n\text{-}x$, and the dimensionality of croaking is x.[92] Therefore, combining these concepts restores the dimensionality of the original event (n). Other parts of speech play similar syntactic roles; for example, definite articles reduce the generality of their associated count nouns.

Hypothetically, this syntactic process that restores the dimensionality of concrete experience is necessary to fully visualize abstract concepts. For example, the visualization of the abstract subject frog_ξ requires seeing the frog's wide mouth and big eyes as it squats on a lily pad. The visualization of the other parts of the sentence further limits the scope of the visualization. For example, green_φ removes the possibility of the frog being brown_φ, and the visualization of the verb croak_ξ prevents the frog from just sitting there, doing nothing.

Applying this process to the original sentence results in four acts of successive visualization:

$$\Psi(\text{frog}_\varphi),\ \Psi(\text{green}_\varphi),\ \Psi(\text{croaked}_\varphi),\ \Psi(\text{loudly}_\varphi)$$

To generalize this process, the original grammar can be extended so that the terminal nodes consist exclusively of sensation, which creates a transformation from sentence structure to the concrete sensory space in which the meaning of the sentence is visualized:

$$S \rightarrow VP\ (NP)$$
$$NP \rightarrow ADJ\ (N)$$
$$VP \rightarrow ADV\ (V)$$
$$ADJ \rightarrow \Psi\ (\Omega\ (adj_\xi))$$
$$N \rightarrow \Psi\ (\Omega\ (n_\xi))$$

---

[92] In the current example, one might let x equal 1 to correspond to the temporal dimension, although x may in general be higher since the VP often carries modality.

ADV → Ψ (Ω (adv$_\xi$))
V → Ψ (Ω (v$_\xi$))

3.8.3.3 Sentences

There are fundamentally two types of sentences:
sentences about events and sentences about identity.

The previous section explored the structure of a sentence about a physical event. A second kind of sentence describes language itself, and is used to define words by expressing relations at a higher epistemic level. The distinction between sentences about the world and sentences about language mirrors a fundamental dichotomy known in many contexts with different terminology: synchronic/diachronic, knowledge/news, *a priori/a posteriori*, synthetic/analytic, *de re/de dicto*, necessary/contingent, etc. Distinguishing between these two types of sentences is vital; to mistake one type of sentence for the other leads to subtle but serious confusion.

Sentences about events can be understood as formulas to dynamically construct zeroth-order concepts, while sentences about language describe higher-order relations. Sentences about language typically take the following form: *word* is a *definition* (or *part* is-a *whole*).[93] Therefore, sentences of this kind should be interpreted as definitions that express (abstract) logical relations, rather than (concrete) contingent statements about the world:

- ◆ Apples are fruits.
- ◆ An apple is a fruit.
- ◆ Apples are red.
- ◆ An apple is a red thing.

---

[93] Although the copula *is-a* is very common in this context, several forms of the verb "to be", the verb "means", and other words can also be used. At least in English, these formulations require that the symbol that is being defined precedes its definition.

111

The underlying structure of these sentences is significantly different from the structure of sentences about events. Consider the example made famous by Helen Keller, who at the age of twenty-one learned her first word: water$_\xi$. Her understanding entailed knowing that the word water$_\xi$ *meant* water$_\varphi$. It is tempting to model this as an association between the auditory word water$_\varphi$ and the physical experience of water$_\varphi$:

water-word$_\varphi$ = water-object$_\varphi$

Although the equivalence relation does not exist in the basic model as an associative link, it can be expressed as two symbols that belong to a common whole, which establishes an equivalence class over those symbols:

whole(ref(water-word$_\varphi$) , ref(water-object$_\varphi$))

The equality between these two concepts is thereby achieved by the introduction of symbols that designate each of them, and a metaconcept which creates an equivalence class that contains the abstract water-object and water-word concepts, which is graphically depicted in Figure 3.8.3c. In this way, metaconcepts equate verbal concepts with their corresponding physical concepts, thus associating word and object.

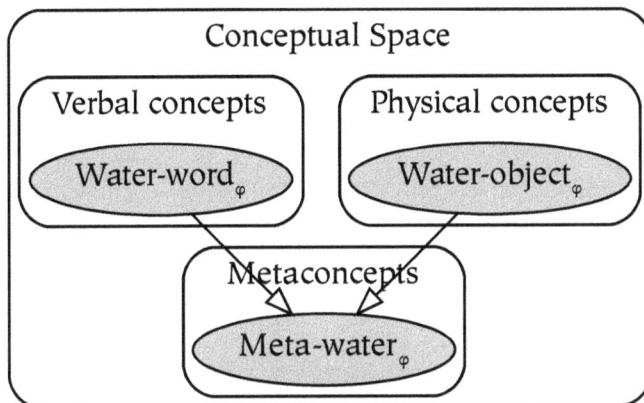

Figure 3.8.3c: The proposed structure behind knowing "water is water".

Part 4

PRACTICAL
IMPLICATIONS

A human being is a part of the whole, called by us "Universe", a part limited in time and space. He experiences himself, his thoughts and feelings as something separated from the rest – a kind of optical delusion of his consciousness. This delusion is a kind of prison for us, restricting us to our personal desires and to affection for a few persons nearest to us. Our task must be to free ourselves from this prison by widening our circle of compassion to embrace all living creatures and the whole of nature in its beauty.

Albert Einstein [Einstein & Sullivan, 1972]

Chapter 9
Concrete and Abstract

Concrete or zeroth-order concepts are wholes of sensation. Because they have the dimensionality of those sensations, they are concrete, open-dimensional events. Similarly, entire sentences that are formulas for constructing zeroth-order concepts result in concepts of the same dimensionality. In contrast, individual parts of speech represent abstract concepts and have only a portion of the dimensionality of sensory events, which is exactly what makes them universally applicable. For example, the color blue would not be able to color all the blue things if it had a particular spatial location.

As another example, take the sentence "She dances beautifully". Most people probably accept that without a dancer of some sort, there can be no dance. Similarly, there can be no dancer without a dance; a dancer does, will do, or has done a dance. The co-occurrence of the dancer and the dance is a necessity; they constitute a concrete whole that corresponds to a complete sentence, that cannot be validly referenced using either a noun (the dancer) or a verb (to dance) exclusively.[94] More poetically, neither a dancer nor a dance has ever existed independently of the other.

As abstract parts of speech are combined, they create concepts that are increasingly concrete. For example, the phrase "she dances" exists more concretely than its subject ("she") or its predicate ("dancing"); the entire sentence is more real, meaningful, or concrete than its noun or verb phrases individually.[95] The physical things that are designated by nouns are abstract concepts that lack a temporal dimension, and thus they cannot form a concrete part of a high-dimensional space (unless those nouns are implicitly or explicitly modified by verbs). Although nouns are meaningful in an abstract sense, their dimensionality is lower than that of physical space because they lack a temporal extent (nouns are abstract precisely because they generalize over the temporal dimension). Therefore, they are dimensionally incomplete, and only concrete concepts are completely meaningful as parts of a high-dimensional space.[96]

The distinction between concrete and abstract can be understood by analogy: although the adjective "quick" has some meaning, it is easy to recognize as incomplete. It begs the

---

[94] In other words, because individual parts of speech are abstract, the complete sentence is the smallest linguistic referent which can be validly dereferenced. For example, even proper nouns (understood as 3-D or atemporal objects) must be combined with a verb to validly refer to an event in the world.

[95] Alternatively, noun phrases and verb phrases are less independent than entire sentences, since things which have both spatial and temporal parts are more independent (or less abstract).

[96] The argument that nouns and verbs cannot be validly dereferenced independently of one another can be made on the basis of physics: the referents of spatial things (nouns) and temporal things (verbs) never exist as separate entities in physical reality, since objects in spacetime require both spatial and temporal coordinates. From a cognitive perspective, they cannot be visualized because they are dimensionally incomplete (although it is possible to imagine a 3-D object not moving, there is an implicit verb in that case: "remaining still").

questions, "Quick what? What is it that is quick?". However, nouns such as "me" are also incomplete and should raise similar questions: "I did what?". Further, nouns are not merely incomplete in terms of sentence structure, but in terms of corresponding to anything concrete[97] (presumably because material solidity is regarded as sufficient for existence under the classical (Newtonian) view of space).

The implications of incorrectly reifying nouns or other parts of speech are both practical and significant. Since desire affects things *as we understand them*, misunderstanding the nature of things renders us less capable of achieving our desires. For example, although we will be unhappy if we like "tasting sugar" but mistakenly seek "tasting salt", we will probably be able to learn from our mistakes in a straightforward way. On the other hand, desiring the wrong *type* of things is a more subtle and pernicious problem. For example, if we like the taste of sugar but end up seeking sugar as a substance, we might collect sugar far beyond the time or capacity that we have to taste and enjoy it, a mistake that is considerably more difficult to detect and correct.

---

[97] Although it would be possible to understand nouns as references to high-dimensional or permanent (4-D) entities, in that case they would not be able to be modified by a verb.

Chapter 10
Identity

The relation of identity is defined under the assumption that events are unique, so by default, no two events are identical. Similarly, all sensations are different: there is always a dimension along which any two sensations differ. However, when sensation is collected into concepts, the symbols that refer to those concepts enable generalization by higher-order concepts. In virtue of that generalization, differences between individual concepts are forgotten, and they become conceptually identical. This nominal identity is not entirely subjective since it captures aspects of truth about the world, but in virtue of forgetting, it does not capture the entire truth about the world.

Because nominal identity requires the association of a symbol and an object, it is invariably approximate. This inexact relationship often manifests in non-obvious ways, such as the paradox of the heap (see [Hyde & Raffman, 2018]):

> *If there is a heap of sand, and grains are removed one at a time, at what point is the heap no longer a heap?*

While it is clear that a heap exists at one point and does not at another, it seems odd that a single grain of sand could make the difference between a heap and a non-heap. If a single grain of sand cannot make such a big difference, then heaps$_\varphi$ and other concepts apply to their objects to varying degrees, which is problematic for anyone who believes that propositions about objects in the world can be fully true or false.[98]

In virtue of generalization, *the same* object can be described in many different and valid ways. For example, the following large-scale and small-scale descriptions of an apple given by people in different lines of work illustrate this point:

♦ **Sociologist**: "The apple is a food-stuff which the proletariat can turn into cider and feed to the masses to keep them from revolting."

♦ **Psychologist**: "The apple often stops the hunger neurons from firing, thus contributing to the cessation of the apple-gathering response."

♦ **Biologist**: "The apple is a fruit, whose sweetness has been selected by evolution to provide for the disbursement and fertilization of the tree's dicotyledonous progeny."

♦ **Chemist**: "The apple is a complex of medium-chain, starchy hydrocarbons. It contains approximately twenty grams of fructose."

♦ **Physicist**: "The apple contains primarily carbon, hydrogen, and oxygen. It warps spacetime in virtue of its mass."

Each statement is only a partial truth with respect to the apple object. The variety of these statements demonstrates that the characterization of an apple depends on an observer's perspective, and that none of these statements provides an

---

[98] This limitation is removed in a variant of classical logic called *fuzzy logic*.

exhaustive account. Even a single observer characterizes the apple differently at different times: the observer-when-hungry categorizes the apple as something to eat, while the observer-when-fed categorizes the apple as merely a fruit. These different levels of description are not inherently exclusive of each other, but only one formulation exists at one time when they are formulated symbolically. In virtue of that, emotions and thoughts often isolate a single story from all of the possible narratives that could be told about an apple.

Chapter 11
Absolute and Relative

Imagine a town in which "... all the children are above average".[99] Although it is a pleasing image, such a town cannot exist; in order for someone to be above average, someone else must be below average. Nonetheless, it serves as an excellent and very explicit example of the relativity of properties.

The properties of an object, such as being average, are either relative or absolute because they are extrinsic (and inessential) or intrinsic (and essential) to that object. In other words, the relative properties of blueberries such as being something that grows on bushes, depend on the relationship of those blueberries to other things. Their absolute properties, such as high fructose content, depend on aspects of blueberry-matter and are theoretically independent of the relationship of blueberries to other things.

---

[99] Garrison Keillor maintains this is true of the town called Lake Woebegone, in the introduction to his radio show, *A Prairie Home Companion*.

However, the distinction between these two types of properties is not always clear; for example, the relative property "eaten by people" is related to the absolute property "fructose content". Ultimately, it may not be possible to completely separate the absolute nature of a thing from all of its possible (relative) interactions.[100]

If all properties are relative, however, things become meaningless. Therefore, one might conclude that only certain properties are absolute, or have a definable essence that is independent of other things. But which properties are absolute? Is the mass of a tree absolute, since it does not depend on the mass of non-tree things? However, the mass of a tree is defined in kilograms, and kilograms are in turn defined relative to the mass of a certain volume of water at sea level.[101] This chain of reasoning seems to indicate that even abstract properties of an object such as its mass are relative to external objects.

The implicit resolution to this issue is that things are relative to one another in virtue of their wholes, while they are absolute in virtue of their parts. Even the *expression* of absolute properties such as mass is relative, however, because expression is necessarily symbolic. On the other hand, our sensory experience of heaviness is inexpressibly unique and experienced absolutely (or in a bottom-up sense).

The philosophy of reductionism makes this identification between parts and the absolute explicit by claiming that relative descriptions are exclusively external (or whole-based) and that absolute descriptions are exclusively internal (or part-based). Reductionism also claims that a thing is fully known when one knows its parts. For example, to understand people and their

---

[100] The latter is roughly what the scientific method seeks to express in a set of conditionals called *experiments*.

[101] At least, the original definition of the kilogram was the mass of a liter of water at sea level. Since that mass can vary, the kilogram was subsequently defined in terms of International Prototype Kilogram, a particular object located in France. Since the mass of *that* object has also been found to vary, the kilogram is currently being defined once again.

behavior, one must study psychology. To understand how psychology works, one must study physiology and the mechanism of the brain. To understand how physiology works, one must study biology and the mechanism of the neurons within the brain. To understand how biology works, one must study chemistry or physics and the mechanism of the molecules and quarks that make up the neurons, *et cetera.*

While there is no question that reductionistic analysis results in a very detailed explanation, it does not necessarily entail an increase in explanatory power. In other words, although a description that uses small parts is more detailed, it may be unnecessarily complicated. Similarly, the operation of the whole is not *caused* by the operation of parts any more than the operation of the parts is caused by the operation of the whole; causation requires that causes temporally precede their effects, which is not the case for spatial wholes and their parts.

Therefore, appeal to microscopic objects is not always necessary (or even beneficial), since movement at a macroscopic level can often be fully described in terms of macroscopic objects. For example, the neural or neuroanatomical description of a person is substantially less useful to most people than a physiological description, since we can more easily make physiological changes like getting exercise than direct changes to our chemical composition. Further, although the microscopic level does offer a more detailed analysis, it substitutes rational and relative thought for intuitive and absolute knowing, which is not always beneficial.

Chapter 12
Negation

Sensation derives meaning by referring to objects; that meaning is absolute in so far as it is not relative to other sensations. Similarly, the bottom-up aspect of concepts is defined by the sensations of which those concepts are composed. The top-down aspect of concepts, on the other hand, is defined relative to other concepts; concepts without sensory input rise to the foreground only when others recede to the background. As a result, concepts formed by a bottom-up process do not have a negation, whereas concepts formed by a top-down process do have a negation.[102]

In other words, what is absolute is regarded as a whole; it is not a part, and therefore it is not relative to some larger thing. Because the absolute is whole and does not have a complement,

---

[102] This is prefigured by the differing use of negation in Buddhist and Western logic: Buddhist logic often uses non-affirming negation, while Western logic emphasizes affirming negation.

therefore it has no negation. Similarly, the reason that conceptual parts *do* have a negation is that they are defined top-down, relative to a larger conceptual space. Specifically, they have complements with respect to the concepts that are their wholes, and those complements form their negations (i.e., with respect to those wholes). Thus, concepts in and of themselves are neither strictly relative or absolute: they are absolute in virtue of the sensation of which they are a whole, and they are relative in virtue of the larger concepts of which they are a part.

At the endpoints of the sensory–conceptual continuum are purely analytical entities that have no absolute aspect (or *negative entities*), and unanalyzed things that have no relative aspect (or *positive entities*). These two types of entities offer an excellent example of the separability of the relative and the absolute.[103]

Negative entities such as a hole$_\varphi$ are defined in relation or relative to other concepts, but they have no (absolute) sensory content of their own.[104] Therefore, holes are known *only* in relation to a larger context; for example, a hole in the ground is known only in virtue of being surrounded by earth.[105] At the other end of the spectrum are positive entities, which are purely sensory or absolute, and therefore do not have a negation. For example, "the negation of a tree" is not meaningful at a sensory level: it does not entail any other sensation, and it is not clear

---

[103] The relation of emotions to these endpoints is particularly interesting, since emotional attachment to negative entities is entirely conceptual and emotional attachment to positive entities is entirely sensory. See [Casati, 2009] or [Reicher, 2019] for a deeper discussion of non-existent or negative entities.

[104] Negative entities are quite similar to the Buddhist conception of self (understood as the "mere I"), in that they exist on a relative level but not on an absolute level. Similarly, one might argue that St Augustine held evil to be a negative entity, for he said that evil did not exist except as a privation of the good.

[105] Therefore, we can say *where* a whole is, but we cannot say *what* a hole is, since a hole has wholes but no parts.

what the not-tree looks like. In other words, there is no such thing as a sensory opposite, since all sensation is positive appearance.[106]

Most entities have both relative and absolute aspects; therefore, the relative aspect of an entity has a negation while the absolute aspect does not. From a subjective point of view, anything is absolute if it is left unanalyzed and experienced purely bottom-up, and anything is relative if it is analyzed and experienced in virtue of top-down influence. More simply, every entity is absolute as a whole and relative as a part.

---

[106] Sensations *do* have a spatial complement (i.e., sensation in other spatial locations), although that space is known only in virtue of subsequent conceptual wholes. Sensory negation may be defined as the lack of any sensation, but this is quite unlike conceptual negation (which entails the conceptual presence of the conceptual complement). Therefore, conceptual negation is called an affirming negative, and sensory negations is called a non-affirming negative.

Chapter 13
Intuition

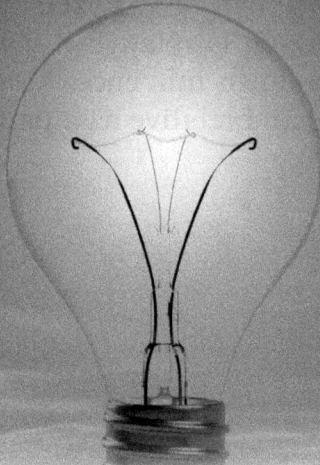

Intuition is not the same as rational thought, but it is not irrational either; it is multi-rational, capable of understanding multiple concepts at the same time. Therefore, intuition is able both to use concepts and to transcend some of the limitations of rational thought. Although intuition is sometimes characterized as nonconceptual since it is non-symbolic, it is more properly characterized as multi-conceptual since it utilizes the content of multiple concepts (just as a picture is worth a thousand words). Because conceptualization is often relatively course, intuition is often associated with sensation rather than conceptualization, although intuition could not represent any mereological relations if it had no part/whole structure.

As opposed to intuition, rational thought is constructed of statements, where each statement has a syntactic structure that corresponds to a single conceptual hierarchy. Although there are exceptions such as puns that may correspond to two or more conceptual hierarchies, most statements are structurally unambiguous. Intuition, by contrast, uses an extremely limited syntax (i.e., mereological parthood without symbols), but it can use *all words at once*. Hence, intuition is a structure which corresponds to a dense mass of mereological and referential relations between multiple, overlapping concepts. Therefore, for the intuitive mind, everything is related to everything else.

Historically, the division between intuition and rational thought has manifested in many ways. Evans and Stanovich, reporting on this division in the context of Dual Process Theory, sum up this situation as follows:

> *The distinction between two kinds of thinking, one fast and intuitive, the other slow and deliberative, is both ancient in origin and widespread in philosophical and psychological writing. Such a distinction has been made by many authors in many fields, often in ignorance of the related writing of others.*

Jonathan Evans, [Evans & Stanovich, 2013].

In the language of Dual Process Theory, intuition is a product of System 1 and rational thought is a product of System 2. In terms of the basic model, System 1 consists of sensation and zeroth-order concepts, while System 2 consists of symbols and higher-order concepts. As System 1 is multi-conceptual and operates in parallel, it cannot be symbolic. Conversely, symbolic processing must happen serially, so System 2 is only capable of conceptualizing a single concept at a time.

The informal argument that System 2 necessarily operates serially is based on inhibition. In particular, the argument from inhibition that symbols must operate serially is that symbols are defined in terms of both the presence and absence of other concepts. In other words, symbols are defined in terms of what they are not, in addition to what they are.[107] Further, the strength of top-down activation must outweigh bottom-up activation,

---

[107] For example, in order to think of a dog, a symbol must inhibit all concepts of non-dog animals; otherwise, the visualized concept will not be sufficiently specific.

otherwise it would be impossible to conceptualize things that are not present. In other words, symbols must be capable of representing and reactivating what they represent in the context of unrelated bottom-up activation, and the way to do that is by strongly inhibiting the negation of that concept.

Type 2 thinking, by inhibiting all irrelevant activation and forgetting numerous other conceptual relations, emphasizes a particular meaning. Therefore, while Type 2 thought is capable of knowing the parts and wholes of a concept, it causes the isolation of that idea by inhibiting its complement.

In contrast, Type 1 knowing does not isolate things in this way; it does not take things out of context or understand things solely in terms of their parts, but rather knows things in relation to everything else; no relations are completely inhibited. Type 1 knowing is therefore not only capable of knowing many concepts about something, but it is capable of knowing those concepts simultaneously (i.e., since concepts do not inherently interfere with one another). Additionally, because conceptual operations are performed in parallel, intuition is *extremely* fast.[108] In fact, the intuitive mind knows so much so quickly that it cannot be adequately described in language. As a result, intuition is often expressed metaphorically, since relating intuitions to one another bypasses the need to define them explicitly. [109]

---

[108] The bandwidth of System 2, because it processes linguistic symbols serially, drastically limits the capability of concepts compared to intuition. However, System 1 tends to be biased in ways which may be undesirable, which leads to its characterization as irrational. See the excellent books by [Kahneman, 2013] or [Gladwell, 2007] for more thorough discussion.

[109] Although the content of intuition cannot be described in language, it is possible to explicitly express how intuition works: the experience is ineffable, but the mechanism is effable.

Chapter 14
Animal Cognition

The differences between animal and human cognition are remarkable given the relative lack of neuroanatomical and genealogical differences.[110] Unfortunately, understanding these differences is inherently difficult for at least two reasons. First, animals are reticent to talk in public, so it is difficult to hear about their experience first-hand. Second, although humans talk voluminously, it is difficult to isolate the aspects of cognition that are uniquely human, other than vague indications of "consciousness" or "language". Therefore, in order to contextualize the theory of animal cognition, it is helpful to have a more general theory about where all things fit; inanimate objects and plants should have a place in the theory as well. Not

---

[110] Animal cognition in this context specifically excludes several species that have demonstrated an ability to form higher-order concepts, such as humans, elephants, dolphins, and some higher primates (see [Koerth-Baker 2010]).

surprisingly, these other forms of life are categorized by the basic model according to their degree of referentiality, or their epistemic level.

At the level of epistemic ground are inanimate objects, which lack the ability to sense or to act. For example, rocks do not sense or react to a neighboring brook in virtue of any internal mechanism or references.[111]

A tree, on the other hand, senses things; for example, it senses the sun, and reacts to that sensation by growing toward it. Thus, the tree may be said to be conscious of itself in the same way as a rock, but it also has awareness of its referents, such as the sun. In terms of the basic model of cognition, plants sense, but they do not conceptualize because they do note have a mechanism by which they can form unitizations. For the same reason, animals with nervous systems can conceptualize things.

To summarize, non-referential (or reflexive) consciousness is something that all things have, referential awareness is something that only plants and animals have, and conceptual awareness is something that only animals have. The further differentiation between animal and human cognition is primarily attributed to the human capacity for words and symbols. The smallest change to the basic model of cognition that is capable of producing this difference is the removal of interpretation (Ω).[112] Removing

---

[111] However, one might argue that the sensation and action of inanimate objects is uniform and described by physical laws, and that rocks have some form of limited consciousness of what it is like to be a rock. Under the assumption that all material things have some form of consciousness, then references are conscious in virtue of their materiality, and are further aware of external things in virtue of being referential. References to references create awareness of awareness for the same reason, and a recursive process that involves references allows recursive awareness. All of these types of knowing are experienced in virtue of matter itself being conscious, but they have referential awareness only in virtue of the representational capacity of a nervous system.

[112] Presumably, removing symbolization exclusively is not sufficient, since it could be replaced with sensation of actions (e.g., self-talk).

interpretation (and possibly also symbolization, as shown in Figure 4.14) from the basic model results in a model of animal cognition that allows sensation and concrete concepts, but not symbols or higher-order concepts. This model predicts that animals may sense, visualize, and to some extent conceptualize in the same manner as humans, but they cannot engage in symbolic thought, and as a result, animal cognition is necessarily concrete.[113]

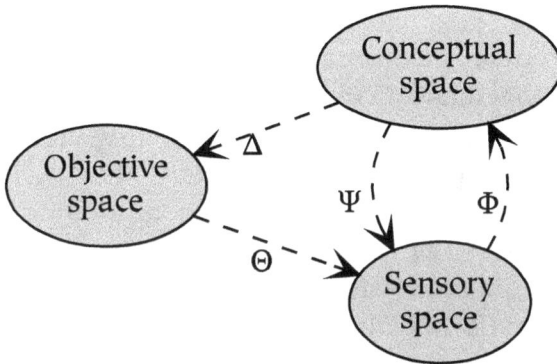

Figure 4.14: Animal cognition, which lacks interpretation (Ω) and symbolization (Ξ).

As symbols enable abstraction, animals can form concrete unitizations but not abstract generalizations, and therefore they cannot think abstract thoughts. Further, they do not experience objects as nominally identical, since identity requires higher-order concepts. This difference in cognitive structure therefore entails differences in what is *a priori* for animals as opposed to humans.[114]

---

[113] The cognitive difference between animals and humans entails that animals are more closely tied to their sensory lives than humans, since their minds operate at a lower epistemic level (i.e. they cannot form abstract concepts).

[114] In particular, truths involving symbols are *a priori* for humans, but not for other animals. However, mereological truths are *a priori* for both humans and animals.

Behaviorally, the lack of interpretation can be understood in relation to the distinction in linguistics between signs and symbols: animals understand words as *signs*, but not as *symbols*. Signs are concrete, and often indicate that something else is impending (e.g., sit_φ, stay_φ, "play dead"$_\varphi$, etc.); they are always embedded in a causal context because they form a single spatiotemporal unit. On the other hand, symbols represent something and can be used to directly activate the concept that they represent.

Symbols enable a dramatic evolutionary advance because they enable the easy formation of recursively constructed concepts, and therefore the creation of linguistic structures of arbitrary complexity (see [Chomsky, 1995]). Linguistically, therefore, while animals may generate and understand certain verbal behaviors, the underlying deep structure of those utterances is significantly different from human syntax. Since the concepts of animals are always zeroth-order, characterizing *how* animal communication is different from human language requires identifying what parts of speech correspond to zeroth-order concepts. The basic model of cognition indicates that animal cognition is formed of entire *sentences*. Thus, what animals lack is the ability to create and comprehend abstract parts of speech such as nouns and verbs. In other words, since animals cannot form concepts corresponding to abstract parts of speech, their sentences are limited to be one word long and to represent entire events.

Expressed slightly differently, the theory of animal cognition proposed here is that animals comprehend the world as composed of events, rather than spatial objects and temporal processes. On a syntactic level, animals comprehend entire sentences, but not parts of speech such as nouns and verbs. This is a direct result of not comprehending space or time as independent entities on a cognitive level (see [Rogers, 1995]). In other words, the concepts of time and space as independent entities in human cognition are only possible in virtue of the abstract generalizations that are enabled by symbolization. Studies of animal behavior reinforce this finding by demonstrating that behavior is unitized, or that learning to perform a given spatial task entails learning both a time and rate at which that task is performed [Gallistel, 1980]. [115]

---

[115] As an interesting consequence, the discovery made explicit by the theory of relativity that space and time are not orthogonal is analogous to undoing the mistaken reification of our abstract higher-order concepts.

Chapter 15
Bottom-Up and Top-Down

Bottom-up and top-down processes in cognition imply a vertical dimension that can be measured using the notion of epistemic level. Sensory parts are responsible for bottom-up activation, and symbolic wholes are responsible for top-down inhibition.[116]

The role of bottom-up processes in cognition is fairly straightforward: concepts are recognized in virtue of sensory input, especially if those concepts are emotionally significant. The role of top-down processes in both what is perceived and how it is perceived is a bit more complicated, and often underestimated.

---

[116] Top-down inhibition is similar to an understanding of how concepts appear to the mind called *apoha theory* that was developed by the Indian scholar Vasubandhu. It is also similar to the spotlight model of attention developed by William James.

As a result of that top-down influence, our perception operates with significant distortion and even creation, an interference that often goes unnoticed. Perhaps this is inevitable, since the cognitive detection of what is not perceived requires extraordinary investigation.

A simple example of bottom-up and top-down effects in the visual system is the phenomenon of *blind spots*, which are areas of the visual field for which there is no sense data. Figure 4.15 can be used to see your blind spots – or better yet, can be used to *not* see them. First, close one eye and look at the dot on the side opposite of your open eye, and move the figure slowly closer and farther from your face. At a certain distance, the dot that you are not directly looking at disappears from your visual field.

●   ●

Figure 4.15: Blind spots.

The blind spot in each eye is created by a small patch of missing retina, medial to the point directly behind the pupil where the optic nerve connects to the eyeball. As a result, there is no sensation from the corresponding part of the visual field. Blind spots demonstrate both that there are areas of reality that we expect to sense that we do not, *and* that we are not aware of this lack of sensation. Further, blind spots are not only sensory holes that we do not see and of which we have no awareness, but are areas of illusion. To more clearly demonstrate this fact, if you pass a pen in front of the blind spot that you identified during the previous experiment, you will not see a hole in the pen; rather, the missing part of the pen is filled in by your mind. Therefore, blind spots are characterized by both bottom-up, sensory deficits and top-down illusions.[117]

These missing bits of sensation and areas of hallucination clearly demonstrate that the world as we perceive it is not the world as it is; our sensations are filtered to make them comprehensible. Although this is not necessarily a bad thing, the lack of awareness of this alteration is problematic. As another example of top-down influence, consider the following question:

What part of your mind are are you using?

Most people who read this sentence see it as identical to the following sentence: "What part of your mind are you using?". As the first sentence is not syntactically well-formed, they are not identical unless the first sentence is mentally altered to conform to our expectations and understanding. This type of correction is often beneficial; for example, it automatically corrects the syntax of ill-formed sentences such as the one above and causes false positive percepts of dangerous creatures. However, it is harmful if it creates a world that always conforms to our understanding and in which we recognize only familiar things, since living in such a world would not enable our understanding to increase.[118]

Dreaming and hallucinations are even more extreme examples of playing a creative role in what we sense. If the dream of a tree can arise without a tree, then no external cause at all is necessary for perception. Although this does not invalidate the more common case in which the tree-sensation arises in conjunction with a tree-object, it does make the relationship between the two more tenuous. As a rather extreme example that a number of philosophers and novelists have used to illustrate this issue, there

---

[117] It seems probable that this top-down illusion is in fact present throughout perceptual space, but noticed only in selective contexts (such as in this example).

[118] In other words, if one does not perceive anything that one does not already understand, then learning is not possible. Therefore, although it seems paradoxical, there is a sense in which greater understanding can be achieved by not understanding (at least temporarily).

is no way to tell if we are dreaming or not when sensations do not depend on the presence of objects.[119]

As these examples illustrate, top-down and bottom-up processing offer both an opportunity to balance and a risk of imbalance. That balance is particularly necessary in contexts such as learning a new activity, since top-down cognition is essential for many activities, but it also hinders expert performance. In such cases, therefore, it is beneficial to be able both to think about things and to not think about things.[120]

---

[119] For example, Zhuangzi dreamed that he was a butterfly, and upon awakening, he could not be sure that he was not a butterfly dreaming he was a man (see [Hansen, 2017]).

[120] In more technical terms, the interference between symbolic and subsymbolic processing sometimes makes it desirable to temporarily stop System 2 from operating so that System 1 may operate without interference. It would be even better if these systems could operate simultaneously without interference, although this may not be possible.

Chapter 16
Attention

Attention is an operation that restricts the domain of perception from an omnipresent awareness to a localized awareness. This selectivity causes an individual to be relatively blind to things outside of the aperture of attention, a phenomenon called *inattentional blindness*.[121] This process is analogous to putting blinders on a horse: although it causes the horse to be less distracted, the horse also perceives less. On a positive note, however, the decreased aperture of awareness allows the horse to more fully analyze what *is* perceived.

Attention is governed by both bottom-up and top-down processing, which gives rise to two types of attention called *stimulus-driven* and *goal-directed* attention, respectively. In terms of the basic model, attention is determined bottom-up by

---

[121] Although some sensation is still processed cognitively, information that is outside of attention is often inaccessible (in the sense of access vs phenomenal consciousness, as described in [Block, 1995]).

conceptualization and top-down by visualization. Bottom-up sensory activation is prone to grab attention if it is particularly intense, unexpected, or emotionally valent. Top-down conceptual inhibition guides attention to what is relevant by inhibiting conceptual wholes outside the scope of attention. As a side effect, top-down attention is limited to concepts that already exist.

Attention has a similar relationship to both concepts and emotions. Just as concepts guide attention and the subsequent scope of attention limits subsequent concepts, attention is also guided by emotion and that scope limits subsequent emotions. In both cases, we are conceptually and emotionally reactive primarily to the content of awareness, and it is attention which in turn governs the aperture of that awareness.

Attention, in addition to being viewed in an impersonal causal chain, is a skill that we are practicing all the time, regardless of whether we are conscious of doing so or not. Training in attention explicitly often entails exercising both its mereological and referential aspects.

Mereological training in attention consists of exercises such as directing awareness to areas of space of of which one is infrequently aware as in body scan meditations, or sustained awareness of a particular location as in meditation on an object. This process happens routinely as a side effect of various activities such as physical exercise or piano practice.

Referential training in attention explicitly directs awareness to different epistemic levels. For example, one may direct awareness exclusively to the occurrence of thoughts or to the referential content of those thoughts, where the latter awareness is of a higher referential level than the former. This type of training figures prominently in various forms of contemplative practice and meditation.[122] In terms of the basic model of cognition,

---

[122] In the type of meditation known as *noting practice*, meditators are often instructed to label their thoughts *as* thinking. That advice is significant in terms of epistemic level, because it implies that one should be aware of thoughts *as* thoughts, rather than engaging with the conceptual content of those thoughts.

meditation that enables one to remain at the epistemic level of concrete concepts develops one's intuitive ability.

Chapter 17
Emotions

Despite the profound importance of emotions, much less is known about them than is known about thoughts.[123] Perhaps this is due to their relative complexity, the tendency of cultures to preserve teachings from higher epistemic levels better than teachings from lower epistemic levels, or to the fact that emotions are not well-suited to being described symbolically.

The cultural dissociation of identity from emotionality is so prevalent that it is encoded in numerous social and legal systems. For example, there is no legal responsibility for actions that are committed "in the height of passion". On the other hand, crimes committed when "thinking too much" are considered premeditated, which increases the amount of responsibility. But if

---

[123] For example, there is no agreement about how many emotions there are, or even where the experience of emotions occurs subjectively; for example, fear may occur in the belly, or stress may occur in the shoulders, although mood is often expressed as an omnipresent phenomenon.

we are responsible for what we think, why are we not responsible for what we feel? One possible answer is that identification with thoughts rather than emotions is an attempt to define ourselves as what we have control over. However, the claim that we have control over what we think about is dubious, because most of us cannot even control whether we are thinking or not. In other words, if one does not have sufficient control over one's mind to start and stop thinking, then how could it be possible to have the fine degree of control required to choose the content of thought?

Historically, the reluctance to scientifically examine emotions is probably related to their antagonism with rational thought. However, the depiction of cognition as consisting of exclusively bottom-up emotions and top-down symbols is an overly simplistic characterization, since emotions play a large role in reasoning, just as emotions have their reasons. Although strong emotions can certainly encourage illogical conclusions, we think certain thoughts as opposed to others precisely because of their emotional valence and their conceptual context.

The role of emotions is particularly complex because they can become attached to symbols, or to references themselves instead of their referents.[124] For example, consider the profound differences between liking the sensation of "peanut butter"$_\psi$, liking the concept of "peanut butter"$_\varphi$, and liking the symbols "peanut butter"$_\xi$.

- Liking the *sensation* of peanut butter means that you enjoy the taste of peanut butter or the mouth feel of dollops smeared on an apple or carrot.

- Liking the *concept* of peanut butter means that you like the concept rather than the experience. Perhaps peanut butter is

---

[124] As the variety of emotions is huge, this section focuses only on two emotions as they relate to the basic model: like and dislike (or attraction and aversion).

good because it is buttery, vegan, and not as expensive as cashew butter.

◆ Liking the *symbol* of peanut butter means that you like the actual symbols (i.e., the words "peanut butter"). Although it may seem odd to like symbols, they may become significant triggers if they are conditioned by their association with desirable and undesirable objects.[125]

The emotional valence of concepts becomes the emotional valence of objects in a process called *cognitive fusion*. Cognitive fusion is an operational hazard of the way cognition works because it causes emotional confusion between concepts and objects (i.e., as a result of the concept inheriting the emotional significance of its referential content). The occurrence of the concept may additionally cause physiological responses that are inherently rewarding beyond the actual experience, such as activation of the parasympathetic rest/digest mechanism. As a result, thinking has the potential to condition concepts even further by creating a feedback loop that does not involve the presence of the object.

At least in some instances, emotional attachment to symbols rather than their intended objects seems to be a mistaken form of cognition.[126] It can certainly be disadvantageous if it biases which thoughts do and do not occur in virtue of how much we like the thoughts themselves as opposed to the content of those thoughts. Evolutionarily, it may be simply a side effect of emotions conditioning sensory space, and symbols making use of

---

[125] Advertisers make use of this fact to create brand-names and logos that literally become delicious.

[126] The thesis that our symbols should *never* become emotionally valent is similar to the spiritual injunction not to become attached to our thoughts. In that context, undesirable emotional attachment can be diminished by developing equanimity with respect to the occurrence of concepts, or temporarily blocked by preventing the concepts from occurring. There are a number of different theories about how this can be done most effectively, such as adopting a stoic view, getting more exercise, or practicing various forms of meditation.

that same sensory space to represent concepts. On a practical level, even if emotional attachment to symbols is not viewed as an inherently negative thing, disentangling the attachment to symbols from the attachment to the concrete phenomena that those symbols represent is a formidable task.[127]

Regardless of one's views on the proper role of emotions with respect to epistemic level, two things are clear and worthy of reflection. One is that emotional attachment to higher epistemic levels in general causes strong top-down influence, which can be disadvantageous. Another is that lack of equanimity with respect to symbols at any given epistemic level causes bias in that top-down influence. The combination of these two, therefore, is especially problematic.

---

[127] This is especially true because the consequence of removing the emotional valence of the referential content itself would be equivalent to removing any intuition. For further discussion of the role of emotion in intuitive wisdom, see the essay on omniscience and universal empathy at [http://theWholePart.com].

Chapter 18
Beauty

Where do we experience beauty? Do we experience it in the space of our bodies, or in a space that is coextensive with the world that we perceive? Folk wisdom holds that beauty is in the eye of the beholder, and psychologists hold that the positive feelings associated with beauty originate in the dopaminergic neurons of the limbic system. Similarly, the world points to us and tells us that our sense of beauty is subjective, or in our heads. However, we experience beauty in the objects of the world, and tell the world that we experience beauty *out there*. If beauty can only be present in a single location, then which location do we choose?[128]

---

[128] Admittedly, this is somewhat of a rhetorical question. As Thomas Nagel stated, "The subjectivity of consciousness is an irreducible feature of reality, and it must occupy as fundamental a place in any credible world view as matter, energy, space, time and numbers." [Nagel, 1989].

This incongruity with respect to the location of beauty is typically taken as evidence for indirect realism, rather than support for the argument that consciousness is extended. In other words, there are objective aspects of sensation that are due to the world and subjective aspects that are due to us, and beauty is regarded as one of the latter.[129] However, these internal references to an external world provide two possible points of view with respect to the location of beauty.

From the objective or material perspective, references are not treated as referential, so the experience of those references is located within the body. This is the predominant view within science as a whole: it views human bodies as parts of larger wholes and minds as collections of references to that larger whole that are contained within the body. Awareness of the external world is enabled by referentially bringing the external world within the brain or body, which is often assumed to be the location of consciousness.

From the subjective or mental perspective, on the other hand, experience is constituted by the content of those references, and as a result, the experience of beauty is located throughout the world.[130] In other words, since we perceive the referential content instead of the references themselves, beauty is located in beautiful objects rather than in the head. Even if the objects are beautiful because of our previous experience with them, then beauty is a relation in the world which we perceive or not in virtue of having that experience.

If both truths are compatible and valid from different points of view, then it would be a mistake to let the concepts of others interfere with our experience of beauty or vice-versa. Therefore,

---

[129] The philosopher John Locke called these the primary and secondary qualities of perception.

[130] While representations may be seen as non-referential parts from an objective point of view, the importance of their location as subjectively experienced should not be discounted: to ignore referential content in an account of the world is equivalent to entirely devaluing mind in favor of matter.

to cease *feeling* that external objects are beautiful because we are told that nothing is objectively beautiful would be a terrible mistake.[131] If we find roses beautiful and someone else does not, all that is entailed is that we have the concepts that allow us to see their beauty because of our experiential history, while others do not.

The question about where beauty resides can be seen as part of a larger question about whether objective space should be seen as the intersection of all subjective perspectives or as the union of all subjective perspectives. For example, it is common to see pine trees as green, and it is less common to see them as beautiful. This is typically taken as evidence that *greenness* is an objective aspect of pine trees, while their *beautifulness* is a subjective aspect. Although there is no question that beauty is harder to define, the further assumption that beauty is purely subjective while green is purely objective amounts to an *intersectional* thesis. According to this thesis, the physical universe is itself entirely devoid of beauty; beauty is merely the subjective judgment of an observer.

The *unional* thesis entails that objective reality actually contains all subjective truths. For example, a pine tree is *both* beautiful and ugly from different yet valid points of view. According to this thesis, each of us knows aspects of a larger, multifaceted truth in which things in the world are *actually* beautiful and ugly from different perspectives. In other words, beauty and ugliness are relations between our perceptions and our prior experience that also exist in the world.

In slightly different terminology, the fact that the objective point of view must be valid for all observers removes beauty and other properties from objective space, because the translation of what is beautiful from one perspective to another is considerably more difficult than moving from one spatial location to another.

---

131 In other words, the conflation of the subjective and objective perspectives may encourage identification with the references (i.e., the body and particularly the brain) as opposed to the referential content of those references (i.e., the subjective universe).

It is worth considering, however, that just as standing in a different location brings some of the subjective observations of different observers into accord with one another, knowing each other's prior experience with the world may bring into accord subjective judgments such as what is beautiful.

Chapter 19
Kindness

To understand intersubjective kindness, consider the following analogy:

> *The right hand looks after the left hand without thinking in a discriminatory way, "I am the right hand. I am taking care of the left hand."*

Thich Nhat Hanh [Hanh, 1998].

This analogy illustrates that kindness to oneself does not require justification; it is completely natural. To better understand *kindness*, it is useful to categorize behavior along two dimensions: self/other and dual/nondual.

Kindness entails that the self/other distinction is *commutative*. For example, if you have a sense of joy when someone else is pulled over for speeding instead of you, your cognition is not commutative with respect to the division between self and other.

This commutativity is captured by various formulations of the golden rule, a rule that holds we should be equally kind to ourself and others. If kindness is not commutative, then it is either *selfish*, in virtue of which you make yourself happy at the expense of others, or it is *otherish*, in virtue of which you make others happy at your own expense.

Kindness can also be understood with respect to dualistic and nondualistic cognition, where duality is seen as the result of using top-down symbolic processing in cognition. Selfishness and otherishness are both inherently dualistic, since it is not possible to consistently and intentionally benefit oneself or another without reifying the duality between oneself and another; therefore, nondualistic selfishness and nondualistic otherishness do not exist (i.e., if one acts without conceptual duality, one may be kind or unkind, but not exclusively with respect to self or other).

Acting with kindness presents different obstacles depending on the presence or absence of duality. The potential hazard of dualistic selflessness is that unconditional love is necessary to unite the self and other, since they exist at a conceptual distance from one another (i.e., dualistically). If that love remains conditional, conceptual dualism is prone to tip the emotional scales in one direction or the other. On the other hand, the potential hazard of nondualistic selflessness is that if the nondualistic stance is a result of ignorance or lack of conceptual differentiation, then attempts to benefit self or other will not be reliably successful.

Because nonduality is difficult to talk about without reinforcing dualism, nondual traditions often express either that everything is self or that there is no self whatsoever. In both cases, the subject/object duality disappears.[132] For example, if we

---

[132] Treating your neighbor with the same level of kindness as you treat yourself is not self-sacrificing if you consider your neighbor to actually be yourself, but neither is it selfish. The lack of a subject/object distinction therefore creates a philosophy that is significantly different from the typical characterization of solipsism.

identify with our body, we might enjoy eating savory foods or feel sad when we hurt. However, if we identify with our family or some other larger whole, then it doesn't matter if we *personally* win a race or have some good thing happen to us, as long as the person who does is a part of our larger group; this is just what it means to identify as a part (of a group), rather than as a whole (of ones bodily parts).

As this discussion indicates, kindness depends crucially on the location of the self/other conceptual boundary. A more nuanced solution might preserve intellectual duality while allowing emotional nonduality; in other words, one should care for both self and other, but not confuse self and other by failing to intellectually distinguish between them. This is difficult to achieve in practice, since a person may have various habitual tendencies of which they are not conscious. For example, one might take too much credit for their own thought, rather than acknowledging the causal role in one's thought of the entities that are perceived or referenced. This situation is similar to a prideful mirror that imagines it is entirely responsible for moving its reflections about, when in fact its (mental) references are causally moved largely by the movement of the reflected entities themselves.

Chapter 20
Overlap

The parts of the world are overlapping and interdependent.[133] Therefore, although the use of mereological analysis to draw boundaries between things is useful, the associated tendency to consistently rely on a single partition of reality into concepts is problematic.

Unfortunately, the cognitive tendency to view the world as consisting of some number of non-overlapping parts is difficult to avoid. A particularly pernicious example of the lack of overlap is exemplified by what Daniel Dennett calls the *Cartesian theatre*, which exists in various explicit and implicit forms (see [Dennett, 1991]). It arises from the view that the brain contains mental representations of the world and that consciousness is the spatially-withdrawn witness of these representations, rather than being something that is unified with them. Unfortunately,

---

[133] Objects are often seen as independent rather than interdependent, perhaps because they become wholes when we pay attention to them.

theories of consciousness that posit an internal witness often involve an infinite regress, since any witness would have to form an internal witness of their own to understand the external representations that *they* witness. More recent philosophical theories hold that consciousness is a kind of field that exists within the brain and encompasses (and has direct awareness of) its representations. But if consciousness occurs in an extended region, why is it necessarily restricted to occurring within the brain? After all, it has not been observed there any more often than it has been observed in the world.

In general, the lack of overlap between concepts is an operational hazard of higher-order cognition; our rational minds necessarily traffic in mutual exclusivity as a result of using higher-order concepts. Although the creation of higher-order concepts out of existing concepts is more efficient than building new concepts out of sensation directly, higher-order concepts are hierarchical, and hierarchy does not represent multiple overlapping concepts very well. Therefore, it is important to balance the convenience of higher-order concepts with the precision of zeroth-order concepts. In light of this cognitive bias against the formation of overlapping concepts, it is necessary to be diligent to recognize such overlap in the world. As a particularly interesting case of overlap, consider the mereological and referential overlap of two people.

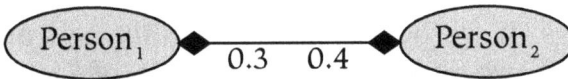

Figure 4.20a: Mereological overlap of two people.

Mereological overlap of two people is shown in Figure 4.20a. This kind of overlap is unusual, because it entails sharing body parts (although it happens in cases of conjoined twins and (arguably) during pregnancy).[134] Referential overlap of individuals occurs if the subjective space of one individual

---

[134] It also happens to some degree when kissing, or in virtue of blood or organ donation.

overlaps the subjective space of another. This is shown in Figure 4.20b, where the numeric subscript denotes a given individual.

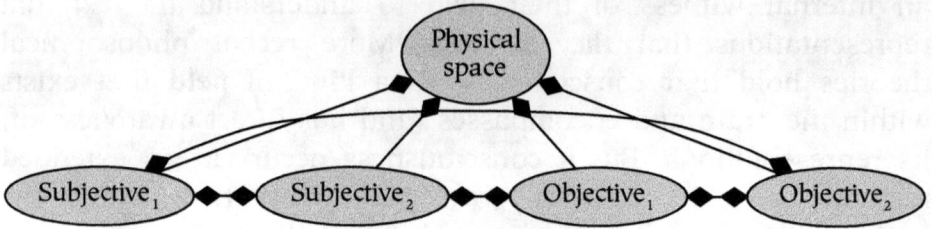

Figure 4.20b: Referential overlap of two people.

Although overlap of bare sensation is trivial because it occurs whenever two individuals see the same thing, the overlap of subjective spaces in general requires that the two conceptual spaces are the same. Thus, it is less clear to what degree the subjective spaces of two individuals are identical. For example, when you perceive a pine cone, and I perceive the same pine cone (from the same physical perspective), do we perceive the same thing? In other words, assuming an identical object, are the appearances of that object identical to each of us?

Because subjective experience cannot be verified by anyone other than the subject, perhaps there is no way to be certain. We might communicate with one another to arrive at an answer, although using communication to verify identity creates further difficulties, since we may use the same words but mean two different things. If we believe that mentality and physicality are tightly coupled, we may use the principle of Occam's razor to argue that two individuals with the same sensory organs and concepts have identical perceptions in response to the same object.[135] In that case, the subjective spaces of two individuals literally overlap because they perceive the same thing, whether in virtue of extended consciousness or internal representation. In more detail, two minds sensing the same object have similar perceptions up to the epistemic level at which a significant

---

[135] Of course, the determination of what constitutes "the same" organs or concepts is also difficult, since it may be assessed materially, functionally, or in some other way.

difference occurs, whether that difference occurs in virtue of different sense organs or subsequent conceptualization. In this way, referential overlap establishes a basis in virtue of which two minds are identical, even if they do not mereologically overlap.[136]

---

[136] In other words, because minds are defined referentially, identity between minds is expressed in terms of referential identity, not mereological identity.

Chapter 21
Self and Other

One of the most important conceptual dichotomies, and perhaps the first concept that we form as children, creates self and other. So how exactly is the concept of *self* defined? The anthropologist Margaret Mead wrote that "self-consciousness is constituted by adopting the perspective of the other toward oneself." [Zahavi, 2008]. This entails that the self is a higher-order concept; it entails not just sensing oneself, but knowing oneself on a relative level as an abstract and enduring object.[137] One's self-identity is often an emotionally laden subject. Therefore, from an emotional point of view, the question "who are you?" is often related to the question "what is the largest whole of yourself that you strongly care about?". In modern

---

[137] Practical assessment of this concept is usually measured using the *mirror self-recognition test,* in which the subject is tested for their ability to recognize their body in a mirror. Passing this test entails that one knows oneself not only "from the inside" or "from the outside", but at an epistemic distance when reflected to oneself.

times, *self* is typically defined as a whole consisting of bodily parts. In older times, the self more often existed only as a part of a tribe. In both cases, however, the differentiation between self and other relies on both mereological distinctions (such as body/world) and referential distinctions (such as subjective/objective).[138] Therefore, the rest of this section explores the notion of self in virtue of how it exists both mereologically and referentially.

A *mereological theory of self* is defined in terms of wholes and parts, and determines characteristics such as the spatial location and size of the self. Several options for the boundary of a mereological self are shown in Figure 4.21a. The location of the self is most often coextensive with the body or a specific part of the body, such as the heart or brain. Mereological theories of self tend to be materialistic, and therefore emphasize connections between objects in physical (or mereological) relation to one another. Mereological theories also tend to deny consciousness, although in modern culture, consciousness and the subjective perspective are more often ignored than explicitly denied.[139]

Of the possible locations of material self-identification, identification with the body is particularly intuitive because it is the largest object that affords relatively consistent sensations while also being contiguous within the field of experience. Contiguity is especially important because it facilitates concept formation; although the body is composed of many parts and is in turn a part of many larger wholes, it is typically viewed as a single mereological whole. As linguistic evidence for this fact, a synonym for person is *individual*, which literally means "unable

---

[138] Another way of expressing the mereological/referential distinction is that consciousness is supported by one physical area, but represents another area, or that its base (or its physical location) is other than its place (or the location in which it is meaningful). See [Ganeri, 2012] for an extensive analysis of this distinction between the base of consciousness (*asraya*) and the place of consciousness (*adhara*) in different philosophical traditions.

[139] For a notable counter example, see writings by Daniel Dennett [Dennett, 1991].

to be divided". The importance of the bodily self in our daily lives and routines is cemented by its use as the legal definition of a person. For example, taking care of the self is a legal mandate in the modern world, while taking care of others is optional (except in the case of one's adolescent children).[140]

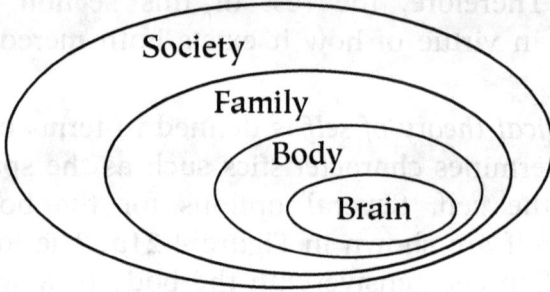

Figure 4.21a: Analysis of the self in terms of parts and wholes.

A *referential theory of self*, on the other hand, is defined in terms of references and referents, and is more closely linked with idealistic philosophies. For example, to identify only at the epistemic level of referents (as opposed to references) leads to identification with what is experienced, rather than with who does the experiencing. Although it might seem strange to identify with the experiences themselves rather than the experiencer, the opposite extreme of exclusive identification with the experiencer is perhaps even more paradoxical, since an experiencer remains unknown unless it is identical with the experience of that experiencer – and on most accounts, it is not. In other words, if you identify as the witness rather than the witnessed, then you do not know yourself from the non-referential point of view, but only at an epistemic distance (i.e., just as you would know someone else).[141]

---

[140] Interestingly, our material possessions are also included in the self-concept from the legal point of view.
[141] The belief that one can know oneself directly, without (dualistic) experience of experience or experiencer, is called self-reflexive or intransitive consciousness. This type of consciousness operates at the physical level of being.

Referential theories of self such as idealism remove this subject/object dilemma by positing that there is no *epistemic ground*, or no material level of being which consists of ultimate referents. As a result of encouraging identification with perceptual content itself rather than the perceiver, this view downplays the distinction between the perception of our bodies and the perception of the world, since the location of the references is less relevant.[142]

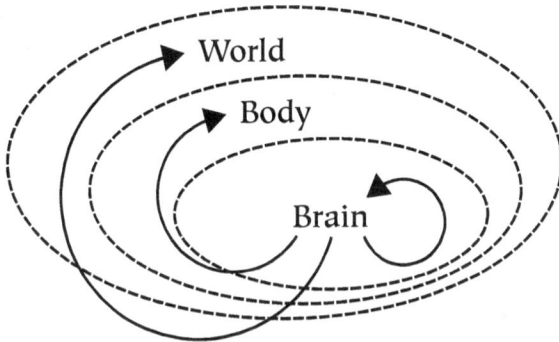

Figure 4.21b: Analysis of the self in terms of references.

Referential identification is illustrated in Figure 4.21b, which depicts a brain as a collection of references to both itself and to a body and world outside of itself. To identify with the references themselves implies a materialistic view and identification with the brain. To identify with the referents of those references implies identification with the referential content of the mind: the brain, body, and world as experienced.

Another way to characterize self-identification utilizes both a *mereological self* and an *epistemic level* at which one relates to that self. For example, one might identify with the bodily self, yet relate to that body in various different ways. This is illustrated in Figure 4.21c, which shows three referential spaces from which one may relate to the bodily self: objective, sensory, and conceptual. The self is viewed within each of these spaces

---

[142] The idealist doctrine was famously summarized by George Berkeley in his statement *"Esse est percipi"*: to be is to be perceived.

differently, as either an object (*body*), a sensation (*body*$_\psi$), or a concept (*body*$_\varphi$), respectively. In other words, even though one identifies with the physical body in all three cases, there is a profound difference in how one acts, feels, or thinks with respect to that body.

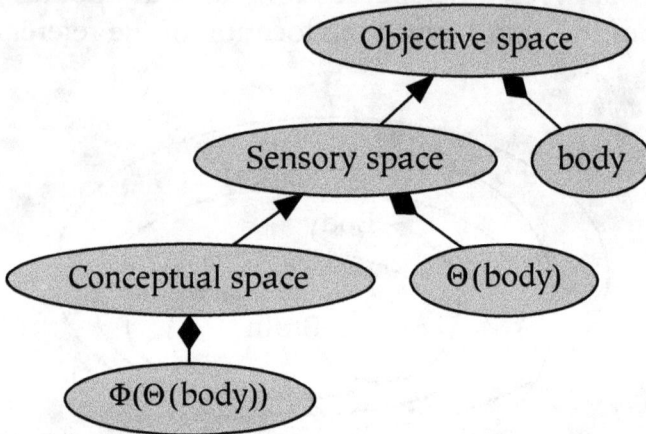

Figure 4.21c: Depiction of bodily (physical) self, sensation of that body, and the concept of that sensation.

Chapter 22
Stratified Self

To some extent, any attempt to define a self may be criticized as trying to identify a complex, concrete entity within a simple, abstract context. For example, the question "Who am I?" uses an abstract pronoun "I", with which we are intended to identify in order to formulate an answer. However, this identification is problematic if it is incorrect to identify with anything abstract in the first place.[143] Refusing to engage with the question is not a good solution, however, since our actions depend on our understanding, even if that understanding is implicit. Therefore, this section explores a stratified self-concept, and attempts to disentangle *where* we are (mereologically) from *what* we are (referentially).

---

[143] For this reason, many spiritual traditions either entirely reject a relative understanding of the absolute, or they caution that a relative understanding of the absolute is not equivalent to our ineffable experience of that absolute.

Boundaries

Although there are many different forms of conceptual dualism, the primary form of dualism is that between self and other. The location of this self/other boundary is contentious because it is not well-defined from exclusively a mereological or referential point of view.

From the mereological point of view, the body/world boundary does not distinguish self and other as entirely different kinds of things. There are no boundaries from the perspective of an outside observer looking inwards; psychology has been exploring the brain for a long time expecting to find the location of consciousness, but it has not found any boundary where one crosses from the material world into the mental world.

From the referential point of view, the body/mind boundary does not distinguish self and other as entirely different kinds of things, either. We cannot experience the world except as it presents to us *through* our bodies, so in some sense we experience the world as our body.[144] Further, a number of psychological experiments show that mind knows body at a referential distance, in the same way that it knows the world. For example, the stories that we tell about the reasons for our own actions are very often wrong, which indicates that we learn and theorize about ourselves and our motivations in much the same way that we learn and theorize about the rest of world.[145]

Since the self/other boundary is not completely and precisely defined either mereologically or referentially, understanding it requires a more sophisticate analysis.

---

[144] Although we *know* that our subjective world is limited, it is not possible to *experience* the objective world without it becoming subjective. For example, we are taught that we are coextensive with our body, but subjectively our senses extend right through our skin; we sense as far as we can in all directions, but can never sense objectivity.

[145] This does not mean that we do not have direct access to subjective sensation, but rather that our subsequent attempts to explain ourselves conceptually are not necessarily a correct interpretation of that direct experience (for example, see [Wilson et al, 1989]).

An Interaction

The mereological and referential perspectives of the self/other dichotomy are illustrated in Table 4.22a, where the mereological body/world distinction creates the columns and the referential body/mind distinction creates the rows.[146]

Table 4.22a: The self/other dichotomy viewed from mereological (body/world) and referential (body/mind) perspectives.

	Body (part)	World (whole)
Body (referents)	$self_a$	other
Mind (references)	$self_b$	$self_c$

From the objective or physical perspective, there is no access to referential content (i.e., $self_b$ and $self_c$ are known only from the subjective perspective). Therefore, as everything is known non-referentially and materially, the distinction between the body and mind of other individuals collapses (i.e., the table becomes one row). As a result, an individual's self is identical to the mereological body from the objective perspective, or $self_a$ and $self_b$ taken as an undifferentiated first column.

From the subjective or mental perspective, referents as material things are initially unknown, and the world is contained within the mind. In other words, there is no *other* from the subjective point of view since there is no *a priori* distinction between body and world in terms of referential level. Therefore, self is initially identified with what is perceived from the subjective perspective, or $self_b$ and $self_c$ taken as an undifferentiated second row.

---

[146] "Mind" in this context entails all subjective referential content, or everything that is experienced.

To summarize these two points of view, the mind is a part of the body from the objective or material perspective, and the body exists within the mind from a subjective or mental perspective. In terms of references, the objective perspective experiences or locates us where the references are located, and the subjective perspective experiences or locates us where the referents of those references are located.[147]

Other as Negative Entity

In Table 4.22a, *other* is a negative entity. It exists in the same way as a hole in the ground; both are things that exist for a given subject on an exclusively conceptual level, neither of which has any sensory content. In other words, there is never consciousness of *other*; it only exists as imputed from higher epistemic levels. However, since there is no experience of *other*, experience of *self* is not relatively meaningful. In more poetic terms, the self/other dichotomy exists at the level of the head (in terms of concepts), but it does not exist at the level of the heart (in terms of sensation). As a result, although neither objective nor subjective perspectives are abandoned, subject/object dualism collapses because the axes cease to be dependent (i.e., they are not orthogonal).

It is an open question how the divisions of different epistemic levels *should* relate to one another. For example, while it may make sense to conceptually discriminate between self and other, to *feel* inherently differently about them may indicate a confusion with respect to epistemic levels. That is, it may indicate an unjustifiable projection of a difference from one epistemic level onto another (i.e., where that difference does not exist in the way in which it was conceived). In terms of Table 4.22a, this entails identification with $self_b$ but not $self_c$, even though we are aware of

---

[147] According to idealism, mind is everywhere and is therefore more open to the idea that the "owner" of a thought is as much the world as it is the individual. As a result, idealism tends to be kinder (because one's mind belongs to others as much as oneself), and materialism tends to be more selfish (since it does not include $self_c$).

both only at an epistemic distance (and in fact, at the same epistemic distance). Even if this projection is not mistaken, a more detailed understanding of how we exist simultaneously on multiple different epistemic levels is sure to be of benefit.

Self as Intersection vs Union

One method to reconcile the objective and subjective points of view allows them to be independent and does not force them into agreement: the objective perspective dictates where the body is and the subjective perspective dictates what the mental experience is. According to this method, self$_b$ in Table 4.22a constitutes an interaction that does not exist except as a mixture of subjective and objective views, a localized and referential self which is valid from neither point of view on its own, and which exists only because the mereological and referential points of view are (perhaps erroneously) forced to share a common terminological *self*.

On the other hand, if the self is regarded as a combination of the body from a mereological perspective and the mind from a referential perspective, then there are two main options to define that combination: self as an intersection or self as a union. The view that the self is an intersection results in the identification of the self with self$_b$ in Table 4.22a. Informally, this view may be expressed as a result of taking the mind to be inside the mereological body *and* the body inside the referential mind. The view of the self as a union results in the identification of the self with self$_{a...c}$. Informally, this view may be expressed by saying that the mind exists outside of the mereological body and that the body extends beyond the referential mind.[148]

Increasing Continuity

Although dualism is often criticized for dividing things, it may also be criticized for not dividing enough, or having an insufficient number of differentiations. To address this criticism,

---

[148] This seeming incongruity may be explained as a failure to correctly translate the notion of the self between the subjective and objective spaces.

the mereological body/world and referential body/mind divisions from Table 4.22a are expanded in Table 4.22b. As before, the columns represent mereological size and the rows represent epistemological level.

Table 4.22b: A stratified view of the self.

	Brain	Body	Neighborhood	Universe
Objective	self^0			
Sensory	self^1			
Concrete Conceptual		self^2		
Abstract Conceptual			self^3	

Table 4.22b illustrates that the notion of self is spread across several epistemic levels and mereological boundaries. In general, the more highly referential the self is (which corresponds to the lower rows of the table), the less localized it becomes.[149] The table may therefore be viewed as a discrete approximation of a continuum from a proximal, dense, and non-referential self to a distal, sparse, and referentially-distant self.

This table also illustrates that the self, which is constituted by the lower-left triangle, is composed of references from multiple epistemic levels. It does not contain any *others*, which exist as the unknown negative entities forming the upper-right triangle.[150] According to this model, the various selves are distinguishable from one another; for example, the sensory self is not the

---

[149] Referents are less localized than their references under the assumption that at least some references point outwards in addition to inwards.

[150] In other words, *other* only exists when multiple epistemic levels are combined into a single self; no self is independently aware of an *other* at its own epistemic level, since that awareness requires an epistemic distance. For example, the "sensory other" is known only as self^2 without the content of self^1. This lack of an other at any given epistemic level puts the self/other dichotomy on a curious footing.

conceptual self. Further, the location of each aspect of self varies. For example, self^1 is located in a body, and self^2 is located in a *perceptual neighborhood*. More generally, the self of each level is located in the same place as its referential content.[151]

The Nondual Perspective

The basic model of cognition is a discrete model of an underlying process that is continuous. Since this work has therefore represented a very discrete or dualistic perspective, it is fitting to end with a note about intellectual continuity, or nonduality.

The term nondualism is sometimes associated with mysticism, but there is nothing mystical about its use in this context, where it refers to the nonduality of subsymbolic mental content. Abstract experience is dualistic or symbolic, and concrete experience is nondualistic or subsymbolic. This does not entail that concrete experience is devoid of concepts, since intuition makes use of conceptual discernment. It does mean, however, that concrete experience is devoid of any *single* dualistic concept at the expense of the others, as happens when that concept is invoked by its symbol. Thus from a psychological point of view, nonduality corresponds to the lack of top-down symbolic inhibition that would otherwise create duality. Therefore, refraining from dualistic thought by preventing too much emotional attachment to symbols leaves space for (relatively more continuous) bottom-up influence.[152]

Of course, this understanding of nonduality is not equivalent to the actual subjective experience of nonduality. The nondual perspective can be embraced only to the extent that it is experienced ineffably or non-symbolically: even structuring our

---

[151] Analogously, my body is mine, but my mind is not (i.e., the "owner" or agent behind the actions of mind is as much the referential content as it is the physical references themselves). In more poetic terms, the thought of the tree belongs as much to the tree as it does to me.

[152] At an even deeper level, nondualism may refer to reflexive or intransitive consciousness, although that perspective is not discussed here.

experience with relatively true notions obscures our lived experience. In other words, we need to *feel* it; no amount of knowing in a relative way can replace experiencing in an absolute way. That said, since both dualistic and nondualistic perspectives are necessary, hopefully the theory explored in this book will help to make the two less polarizing.

As the Zen master Dogen wrote in his well-known summary of a similar process:

To study the self is to forget the self.

To forget the self is to be actualized by myriad things.

When actualized by myriad things, your body and mind as well as the bodies and minds of others drop away.

Dogen Zenji [Dogen et al., 2013]

Conclusion

It seems that in a conclusion, people generally summarize the book and talk about the future. If you've read the book, you don't need a summary, so let's talk about the future.

Personally, I can't see the future; perhaps some of you can. Maybe it doesn't matter, since you can't change the future that you've seen; if you could, that would imply that what you saw was not the future. Further, if you try to change an unavoidable future, you will likely play a causal role in the outcome you were trying to avoid.[153] So I guess the best that I can do is to express my hope.

I hope that after reading this book, some of the numerous ways in which our intellectual understanding affects our lived experience are more clear. I hope also that the basic model of cognition will be beneficial, particularly with respect to understanding our minds and their context in the world. I have tried not to be heavy-handed about it, but I strongly believe that people are more interconnected than many of us realize, and I also believe that undoing any linguistically or culturally transmitted sense of isolation goes a long way in allowing our hearts and minds to open, and in enabling us to more easily recognize the wholes of which we are a part.

May it benefit all beings,

   ~alec

PS: I hope that reading this book has been both enjoyable and intellectually stimulating, and I apologize for any mistakes I have made or any ignorance I have unwittingly transmitted.

---

[153] This becomes particularly poignant if you act unethically in the course of trying to prevent an outcome you believed would happen.

Acknowledgments

I would like to thank all of the people and things that made this book possible:

To all of my professors at various colleges and universities, and especially to those supporting my thesis and other academic works.

To Angelica Kaufmann, Cathy McMahen, Ken Parker, and others for their astute observations and excellent editing.

To my family, for the immeasurable kindness they have shown over the years.

To my lovers, for whom I always tried to be better even though they said that was part of the problem.

To my friends, who have encouraged me to open my heart and lift my gaze.

To my coworkers, for both the opportunity to work with them and the walks after lunch.

To my computer, even though we have a bit of a stormy relationship, and all the wonderful open-source software, such as Inkscape, Graphviz, and Gimp (and also to Scrivener).

Last but not least, to nature, hot yoga, bike rides, pints of nondairy ice cream, and the many other things that kept me going during the difficult times.

Ultimately, SDG.[154]

---

[154] For what its worth, I'm a pantheist, so scientists and earth-worshippers should feel included in this, too.

Appendix A

Formal Summary

Formal equations corresponding to the basic model, to mereology, and to logic.

This appendix is divided into three main parts:

1. A summary of the basic model of cognition.
2. Zeroth-order (mereological) logic.
3. Higher-order (symbolic and abstract) logic.

These parts may be seen as stages, each of which is developed out of its predecessor; the basic model gives rise to mereology, and mereology gives rise to symbolic logic. This introduction summarizes the motivation behind this formulation by introducing relevant aspects of topology, mereology, and logic.

Overview

One of the main endeavors of this book is to explore the aspects of our experience that are due to the nature of our minds. To do that, it is helpful to determine what can be known independently of the world, or *a priori*. By identifying and then removing what we contribute to our experience, we can know the world better as it is.

The basic model of cognition relies on the theories of mereology and reference to describe both how our minds are situated in the world and how in turn our minds give rise to mereology and reference. The choice of mereology is motivated by the fact that the existing symbolic formalisms of mathematics and logic run counter to our intuition about the world. In particular, the most common forms of topology and logic work best only when applied to the abstract geometric and symbolic atoms they take as primitive. As Einstein noted:

> *Geometry [...] is not concerned with the relation of the ideas involved in it to objects of experience, but only with the logical connection of these ideas among themselves.*

Albert Einstein [Einstein, 1924]

On one hand, it is clear that abstract sciences *cannot* involve objects directly, since symbols are inherently abstract and cannot be made concrete without losing their linguistic usefulness. However, geometry and logic are used precisely for their ability to describe real-world scenarios, so it is essential that they fit the world *as well as possible*. The proposal here is to use mereology as a basis for both symbolic logic and topology, in order to take better account of physical objects (which are clearly not composed of zero-dimensional points). To do so, *high-dimensional objects* are introduced as mereological primitives, which form a subsymbolic foundation. That foundation is augmented with (nominal) references to create symbols that allow the creation of abstract low-dimensional entities, such as geometric primitives. Beginning with high-dimensional objects is motivated by the following observations:

- Point-free topologies such as mereotopology are necessary for a subsymbolic model of mind, since point-set topology is inherently atomistic due to its dependence on partless points. In other words, mathematical models of cognition that require everything to have a symbolic description do not leave room for the ineffable, and therefore they are poor models of intuition.

- Mereotopology as a mathematical model of mind provides an excellent fit for human cognitive development. Further, it is clear that geometric thought precedes algebraic thought during the course of development.

- Purely reductionistic or point-based approaches do not make good psychological models, as cognitive science clearly demonstrates that our minds consist of both bottom-up and top-down processes.[155]

Some people might argue that logic and topology do not need to be cognitively or intuitively correct, since they work *in practice*. However, if they are used as models of reality, they will inevitably produce an error of the type this book has argued against: treating objects as if they were equivalent to our

---

[155] In other words, cognitive psychology has no need for points except as abstractions, although it relies rather crucially on basic categories and medium-sized objects.

symbolic representations of them. Therefore, any reduction of this type of mismatch (i.e., by using a non-atomistic model) will be beneficial for both thinking about and interacting with reality.

Topology

The most common form of topology is called point-set topology, and was the branch of mathematics that first succeeded at *enumerating the continuum*. The desire behind this enumeration was the unification of concrete, continuous space and abstract, discrete points. To do so, continuous N-D spaces are defined as infinite numbers of points of zero-size. While there is nothing inherently *invalid* about this approach, it is problematic from a psychological point of view because neither space nor matter is symbolic.[156]

A classic example of one of the problems associated with the use of points as a concrete rather than an abstract formalism arises because the points that divide two shapes must belong to either one or the other of those shapes. A shape that contains the points on its surface is called *closed*, while a shape that does not contain its surface points is called *open*. The problem is that two open shapes can never come into contact with one another because neither can contain the points on their common boundary. Similarly, two closed shapes cannot come into contact, because between any two points on their respective surfaces are an infinite number of other points. While this lack of contact may be regarded as a mere intellectual curiosity, objects in the world are, in fact, connected. Therefore, this problem cannot be ignored by any model of reality that claims to be accurate.

Mereology

Mereology is a nominalistic version of set theory that was developed by the Polish mathematician Stanislaw Lesniewski.

---

[156] In psychological terms, what point-set topology does is completely replace the absolute with the relative by using abstract concepts to approximate concrete reality. To do so, point-set topology requires the use of a completed infinity, which involves a number of problems.

The operation of reference in the current work is roughly equivalent to Lesniewski's naming operator (ε). Historically, mereology was viewed as a mathematical contender to *set theory*, a mathematical formalism for collections of things due primarily to the German mathematician Ernst Zermelo. A mathematical set can be implemented in the basic model by combining two operations, *reference* and *whole*. In fact, the operation of *whole* is the primary reason that mereology is an excellent fit for subsymbolic cognition; while *set* is an intransitive and discrete operation, *whole* is both transitive and continuous.

In mereotopology, which is the science of mereology applied to topology, it is often assumed that parts have the same dimensionality as their respective wholes. In the version of mereotopology developed here, the universe in which topological analysis begins is continuous and open-dimensional. The combination of these two premises seems to suggest that mereotopology does not allow points and lines; however, they are permitted in a nominal sense, as abstract entities. For example, zero-width points on an interval are nominal <u>boundaries</u>: they do not constitute that interval, but merely divide it. The situation is analogous to using a sharp knife to cut a loaf of bread in half: there is no part of the loaf which is not displaced to one side or the other by the knife. Although the location of the cut may be given a name (e.g., "0.5"), there is no bread associated with it. In mereotopology, therefore, real numbers are understood as *nominal boundaries*, or a collection of names for the divisions of an interval, rather than entities which constitute that interval.[157]

Points cannot be divided; therefore, point-set topology begins with points, which are the smallest objects it will ever know, and uses *sets* to construct a universe from those points. This approach is not valid from a psychological perspective because mental space does not have a smallest element out of which other things

---

[157] In other words, numbers (and in fact all abstractions) are <u>negative entities</u> rather than parts of the space that they divide. As a result, partless particles and completed sets with infinite cardinality are not necessary, although they may be used if desired.

are built; it is always possible to imagine something smaller.[158] For the same reason, the complementary topological approach that begins with the largest possible object and divides it is also invalid. Therefore, the version of mereotopology presented here starts in the middle, taking arbitrary *spatiotemporal volumes* as primitive, and uses them to create unions and intersections as necessary.

As opposed to points, the objects that mereotopology takes as primitive are neither infinitely small nor singular. They are concrete by definition and are linguistically better represented by mass nouns than count nouns. As there is no requirement to have partless parts or wholeless wholes, space is assumed to be both continuous and unbounded (i.e., open above and below). Therefore, mereotopology is inherently neither holistic nor reductionistic, and it analyzes objects just as cognition does: by examining them in terms of both their smaller parts and their larger wholes. Using a set of medium-sized objects as a starting point for analysis underscores another facet of psychological compatibility: such a starting point is constructive, in the same way as mental development itself (i.e., medium-sized objects are *epistemically prior* to both atoms and universes). Therefore, objects are always unknown to some degree, in that their parts and wholes are never fully specified.[159]

As the aim of the version of mereotopology developed here is to be a good fit for cognition, it does not follow a standard mereological development. For a more formally rigorous theory, see GEMTC as developed by Roberto Casati and Achille Varzi

---

[158] This is not an ontological claim about neurons, but rather an epistemological claim about experience.

[159] The fact that the primitives are to some degree unknown may make mathematicians uncomfortable, but it is clearly more compatible with psychological development. Since objects are not fully known geometrical primitives or logically singular subjects, they can only be described in virtue of their interaction with other objects, which describes both what and where they are *relative* to other objects.

[Casati & Varzi, 1999]. For a thorough overview of mereological systems, see the book by Peter Simons [Simons, 2000].

Logic

The reason that a model of cognition requires subsymbolic logic can be demonstrated with the following proposition:

The soccer ball is white.

The problem is that this statement is neither true nor false, since some parts of a soccer ball are white and other parts are not.[160] Symbolic logic, however, requires the subject "soccer ball" to be singular; it is not allowed to have parts (or at least, the subject is necessarily treated as a singular and partless whole by any predicates). In other words, predicates require a symbolic subject in order to yield an all-or-none, true-or-false answer. Therefore, traditional symbolic logic does not work for objects that are continuous. On the other hand, mereological logic allows predicates to be applied to continuous shapes in addition to discrete symbols, so it provides a better fit for actual objects.[161]

---

[160] Equivalently, it is both true and false.

[161] Mereological logic shares some features with a type of logic called intuitionistic logic, but that foundation is not used because it is sufficiently different in both motivation and practice. It is also similar to fuzzy logic, although fuzzy logic expresses *possibility*, rather than parthood. While combining the mereological approach with fuzzy logic would approximate human reasoning better by expressing degree of certainty, that approach is not followed here for brevity.

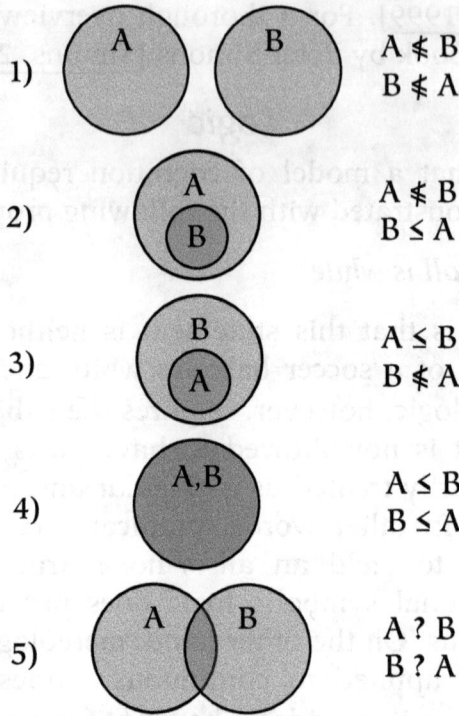

Figure Aa: The five mereological relations.

In order to illustrate the continuous nature of mereotopology, consider again the five mereological relations presented in section *Mereological Space* (p. 20), depicted in Figure Aa. The fifth case is problematic because it cannot be described using classical logic and the parthood relation, unless a new symbol is introduced to name the region of intersection. Intuitively, however, it is clear that A and B overlap; they are parts of each other *to some degree*, and to a complimentary degree, they are not parts of one another.

Table Ab: Shape Logic

Case	A ≤ B	B ≤ A
1	0	0
2	0.3	1
3	1	0.3
4	1	1
5	0.2	0.2

Table Ab is a *truth table* that illustrates how mereological logic gives a complete description of the situation in Figure Aa, where *true* is denoted as 1 and *false* is denoted as 0. The first column of row (5) can be read as "20% of A is a part of B and 80% is not". This solution is therefore an improvement over symbolic logic because it accounts for the overlap in case (5) without having to explicitly refer to the entity created by the intersection, and therefore it avoids unnecessary symbolic proliferation.

The formula that describes parthood as a continuous function of x and y that yields a value between zero and one is:

$$x < y = \frac{|x \cap y|}{|x|}$$

A.1 The Basic Model

The basic model of cognition is a foundation for mereology and symbolic logic.

The set of equations that corresponds to the basic model of cognition are developed according to the following guidelines:

♦ A developmental or constructive approach is followed as much as possible. The model is constructive in that it begins with a universe constituted by some number of objects that create sensations. Conceptual wholes are created by taking unions of these sensory features, and parts are created by taking intersections.[162]

♦ Theoretic devices such as axiomatic reduction are not attempted without psychological motivation, since the primary purpose of the model is to describe cognition.

♦ The details of psychological implementation are omitted, since they would interfere with creating a model that is easily understood.

♦ The desired outcome of becoming familiar with the model is a clarification of thought.

---

[162] As a result, the creation of proper wholes requires at least two parts, and the creation of proper parts requires at least two wholes.

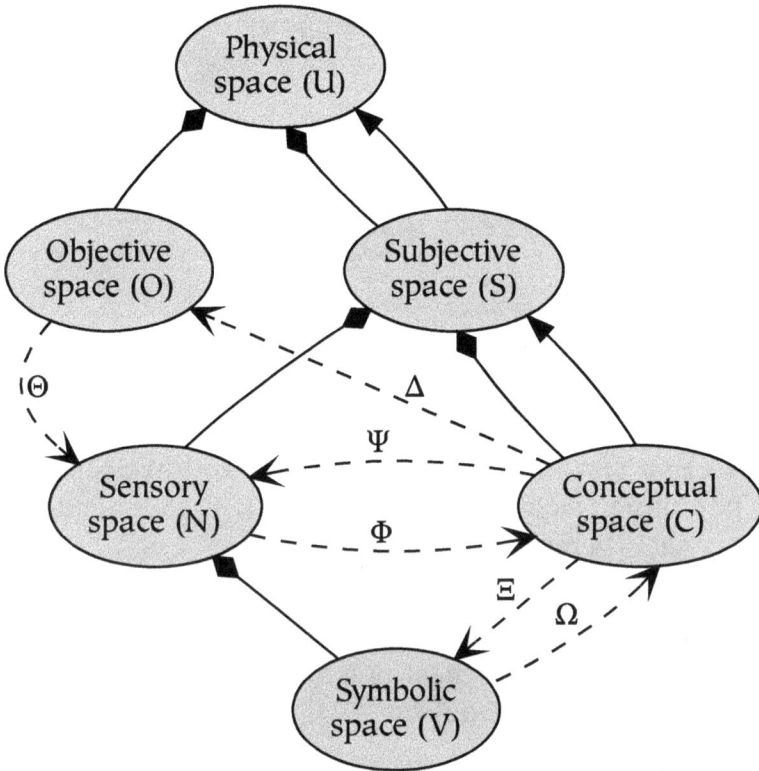

Figure A.1: The basic model of cognition, with sensation (Θ) and action (Δ) mapping to/from subjective subspaces.

Universes

- **Physical space (U)** is reality, or the physical universe. Its parts are called *events*.

- **Subjective space (S)** is everything in physical space that is experienced by a given individual. Its parts are called *experiences*.

- **Conceptual space (C)** is everything within an individual's subjective space that is conceptualized by that individual. Its parts are called concepts.

- **Objective space (O)** is the space within physical space that is not subjectively experienced (i.e., it is independent of the observer). Its parts are called *objects*.

- **Sensory space (N)** is the space within a subjective space that is composed of all subjective experience that is not conceptual, such as sensations and emotions. It is composed of *sensation* or sense data.

- **Symbolic space (V)** is the subspace of sensory space that consists of references to concepts. Its parts are called *symbols*.

Equation 1.1: Physical Space

$$U$$

$$U = O_i + S_i$$

The basic model begins with the physical universe (U).

Physical space is equivalent to the combination of the subjective (S_i) and the objective (O_i) spaces of a given individual (i).

Equation 1.2: Subjective Space

$$S_i \triangleq \forall x_i : \text{reference}(x_i, U)$$
$$S = N + C$$

Subjective space (**S**) is defined to be all references to physical space from a given individual's perspective (*i*).

Subjective space is equivalent to the union of an individual's sensory (**N**) and conceptual (**C**) spaces. In this and the following equations, the perspective of a particular individual (*i*) is assumed.

Equation 1.3: Objective Space

$$O \triangleq U - S$$
$$O_{t+1} = O_t + \Delta(C_t)$$

Objective space (**O**) is defined to be that part of physical space (**U**) which is not subjective space (**S**).

Objective space is the result of action (**Δ**).

Equation 1.4: Sensory Space

$$N \triangleq S - C$$
$$N_{t+1} = N_t + \Theta(O_t) - \Psi(C_t)$$

Sensory space (**N**) is defined to be that part of subjective space (**S**) which is not conceptual space (**C**).

Sensory space is the result of bottom-up sensation (**Θ**) and top-down visualization (**Ψ**).

Equation 1.5: Conceptual Space

$$C \triangleq \forall x : \text{reference}(x, N)$$
$$C_{t+1} = C_t + \Phi(N_t) + \Omega(V_t)$$

Conceptual space (**C**) is defined to be all references to sensory space (**N**).

Conceptual space is the result of conceptualization (Φ) and interpretation (Ω).

Equation 1.6: Symbolic Space

$$V \triangleq \forall x : \text{reference}(x, C)$$
$$V_{t+1} = V_t + \Xi(C_t)$$

Symbolic space (V) is composed of references to conceptual space (C).

V is the result of symbolization (Ξ).

Relations

- **Sensation (Θ):** Sensation is a *causal* function. It changes **N** as a result of **O**.

- **Action (Δ):** Action is a *causal* function. It changes **O** as a result of **C**.

- **Conceptualization (Φ):** Conceptualization is the *whole* function. It creates increasingly conceptual wholes as one moves from **N** to **C**.

- **Visualization (Ψ):** Visualization is the *part* function. It creates increasingly sensory parts as one moves from **C** to **N**.

- **Interpretation (Ω):** Interpretation is the *referent* function. It activates referents in **V** in virtue of symbolic references in **N**.

- **Symbolization (Ξ):** Symbolization is the *reference* function. It activates symbolic references in **N** in virtue of referents in **V**.

Equation 1.7: Sensation

$$\Theta \triangleq \text{cause} : O \mapsto N$$
$$\Theta = \sum_i \Theta_i$$
$$\Theta_i(x) = x_\psi$$

Sensation (Θ) is a causal function that maps from **O** to **N**.

Sensation may be written as the sum of smaller acts of sensation (Θ_i).

An act of sensing (Θ_i) produces a sensation (x_ψ) from an object (x).

Equation 1.8: Action

$$\Delta \triangleq \text{cause} : C \mapsto O$$

$$\Delta = \sum_i \Delta_i$$

$$\Delta_i(x_\varphi) = x$$

Action (Δ) is a causal function that maps from **C** to **O**.

Action may be written as the sum of smaller acts (Δ_i).

An act (Δ_i) produces an object (x) from a concept (x_φ).

Equation 1.9: Conceptualization

$$\Phi \triangleq \text{whole} : N \mapsto C$$

$$\Phi = \bigcup_i \Phi_i$$

$$x_\varphi = \Phi_i(y_{\psi 1}, y_{\psi 2}, \dots) , \quad x_\varphi = \Phi_j(z_{\varphi 1}, z_{\varphi 2}, \dots)$$

Conceptualization (Φ) is the *whole* function, that maps from **N** to **C**.

Conceptualization may be written as the union of smaller acts of conceptualization (Φ_i).

An act of conceptualization (Φ_i, Φ_j) produces a concept (x_φ) from some number of sensations (y_ψ) or concepts (z_φ).

Equation 1.10: Visualization

$$\Psi \triangleq \text{part} : C \mapsto N$$

$$\Psi = \bigcap_i \Psi_i$$

$$\Psi_i(x_{\varphi 1}, x_{\varphi 2}, \dots) = y_\psi , \quad \Psi_j(x_{\varphi 1}, x_{\varphi 2}, \dots) = z_\varphi$$

Visualization (Ψ) is the *part* function, that maps from **C** to **N**.

Visualization may be written as the intersection of smaller acts of visualization (Ψ_i).

An act of visualization (Ψ_i, Ψ_j) produces a sensation (y_ψ) or concept (z_ϕ) from larger conceptual wholes (x_ϕ).

Equation 1.11: Interpretation

$$\Omega \triangleq \text{referent} : V \mapsto C$$
$$\Omega_i(x_\xi) = x_\phi$$

Interpretation (Ω) is the *referent* function, that maps from **V** to **C**.

An act of interpretation (Ω_i) produces a concept (x_ϕ) from a symbol (x_ξ).

Equation 1.12: Symbolization

$$\Xi \triangleq \text{reference} : C \mapsto V$$
$$\Xi_i(x_\phi) = x_\xi$$

Symbolization (Ξ) is the *reference* function, that maps from **C** to **V**.

An act of symbolization (Ξ_i) produces a symbol (x_ξ) from a concept (x_ϕ).

Equation 1.13: Epistemic Level

$$\text{level}(U) \triangleq 0$$
$$\text{level}(\Theta(x)) \triangleq \text{level}(x) + 1$$
$$\text{level}(\Delta(x)) \triangleq \text{level}(x) - 1$$
$$\text{level}(\Phi(x)) \triangleq \text{level}(x) + 1$$
$$\text{level}(\Psi(x)) \triangleq \text{level}(x) - 1$$
$$\text{level}(\Xi(x)) \triangleq \text{level}(x) + 1$$
$$\text{level}(\Omega(x)) \triangleq \text{level}(x) - 1$$

The epistemic level of a thing is the total number of epistemic operations that must be taken in order to reach ground.

Equation 1.14: Conceptual Order

$$\text{order}(\mathsf{U}) \triangleq 0$$
$$\text{order}(\Theta(x)) \triangleq \text{order}(x)$$
$$\text{order}(\Delta(x)) \triangleq \text{order}(x)$$
$$\text{order}(\Phi(x)) \triangleq \text{order}(x)$$
$$\text{order}(\Psi(x)) \triangleq \text{order}(x)$$
$$\text{order}(\Xi(x)) \triangleq \text{order}(x) + 1$$
$$\text{order}(\Omega(x)) \triangleq \text{order}(x) - 1$$

The conceptual order of a concept or sensation increases according to the number of symbolizations required for its construction. It is analogous to referential level.

A.2 Zeroth-Order Logic

Zeroth-order logic is implemented using mereology and reference.

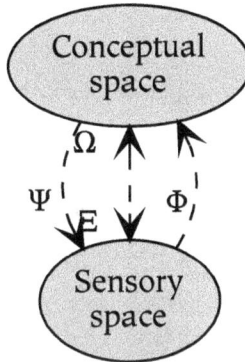

Figure A.2: *a priori* cognition.

The *a priori* operations of the basic model correspond to *part* (Ψ), *whole* (Φ), *reference* (Ξ), and *referent* (Ω). All of these operations are used on the right-hand side of the definitions in zeroth-order logic to produce variables on the left. The *use* of references created with the referential operator (Ξ) as variables on the right-hand side of definitions, however, requires higher-order logic.

195

The transition from basic model operations to logical values is made by defining zeroth-order truth as being *real*: a thing is true *to the degree* that it is a part of the universe. That degree is represented by a continuous truth value between 0 and 1, as described in the section *Logic* at the beginning of this appendix. In terms of visualization, a continuous version of parthood can be written as:

$$Pxy \triangleq \frac{|\Psi(x,y)|}{|\Psi(x)|}$$

x is a part of y (or Pxy) in proportion to the visualization formed by x and y as a fraction of the visualization of x.

For simplicity, however, the truth values that are used in the following section are binary (i.e., following Boole, they are *true* and *false* instead of continuous values; see [Boole, 2003]). Therefore, parthood is written as:

$$Pxy \triangleq \Psi(x,y) = \Psi(x)$$

As a final note, all variables (e.g., x and y) in the following equations are assumed to be concepts, so the subscripts indicating conceptuality are omitted (i.e., it is implied that $x = x_\varphi$ and $y = y_\varphi$ unless otherwise indicated).

Mereology

- **Visualization (Ψ):** Given some number of entities, their intersection creates a part.
- **Conceptualization (Φ):** Given some number of entities, their union creates a whole.

Equation 2.1: Part

$$Pxy \triangleq \Psi(x, y) = \Psi(x)$$

x is a part of *y* if the visualization of *x* and *y* (which is their intersection) is equal to the visualization of *x* (i.e., the intersection of *x* and *y* removes nothing from *x*).

Equation 2.2: Whole

$$Wxy \triangleq \Phi(x, y) = \Phi(x)$$
$$\triangleq \Psi(y, x) = \Psi(y)$$

x is a whole of *y* if the conceptualization of *x* and *y* is equal to the conceptualization of *x* (i.e., the union of *x* and *y* adds nothing to *x*).

Similarly, *x* is a whole of *y* if and only if *y* is a part of *x*.

Equation 2.3: Everything

$$\text{everything}_\psi \triangleq \sum_i x_{\psi i}$$
$$\text{everything} = \bigcirc$$

Everything$_\psi$ is defined as the combination of all possible sensations.

Everything can be written with the *circle* symbol (as with other entities, the lack of a subscript indicating epistemic level indicates that the entity is non-referential, or of epistemic level 0).

Equation 2.4: Truth

$$\text{true}(x) \triangleq Px\bigcirc$$

At a mereological level, truth is equated with being real, or a part of everything. As a result, false or unreal things disappear when they are visualized (i.e., they are <u>negative entities</u>). Mereological truth is a continuous form of truth, so x is true to the degree that all parts of x are parts of everything.

Reference

♦ **Symbolization (Ξ):** Given an entity, a reference to it can be obtained by symbolization.

♦ **Interpretation (Ω):** Given a reference, its referent can be obtained by interpretation.

Equation 2.5: Reference

$$Rxy \triangleq x = \Xi(y)$$

x is a reference to *y* if *x* is produced by symbolizing *y*.

Equation 2.6: Referent

$$Tyx \triangleq y = \Omega(x)$$

y is the referent of *x* if *y* is produced by interpreting *x*.

Basic Operations

Equation 2.7: Negation

$$\neg x \triangleq \bigcirc - \Psi(x)$$
$$\text{false}(x) \triangleq \text{true}(\neg x)$$

The negation of a variable is its sensory opposite.[163]

The falsity of a variable is the truth of that variable's negation.

Equation 2.8: Conjunction

$$x \wedge y \triangleq \text{true}\big(\Phi(x, y)\big)$$

The conjunction of two entities is the truth of the concept that combines both.

Equation 2.9: Disjunction

$$x \vee y \triangleq \text{true}\big(\Phi(\Psi(x), \Psi(y))\big)$$

The disjunction of two entities is the truth of the concept that combines the visualization of each.

Equation 2.10: Proper Part

$$PPxy \triangleq Pxy \wedge \neg Pyx$$

x is a proper part of y if x is a part of y and y is not a part of x.

Equation 2.11: Referential Level

$$Rxy \implies \text{level}(x) = 1 + \text{level}(y)$$

The referential level of a reference is one higher than the referential level of its referent.

---

[163] This refers specifically to affirming negation; non-affirming negation, which removes all certainty from a truth value, is not depicted because it requires the truth value to become more complex.

Equation 2.12: Dimensionality

$$Wxy \wedge \neg Ry \implies \dim(x) = \dim(y)$$
$$Wxy \wedge Ryz \implies \dim(x) = 1 + \dim(z)$$
$$\dim(\bigcirc) = \lim_{n \to \infty} n$$

The dimensionality of a part that is not a reference is equal to the dimensionality of its whole.

The dimensionality of a whole of references is one more than the dimensionality of the referent of that reference.[164]

The dimensionality of the universe is limitless.

Equation 2.13: Mereological Context

$$\text{context}(x) \triangleq \forall z : z = x \vee Pzx \vee Wzx$$

The mereological context of a concept is the concept itself as well as all conceptual parts and wholes of that concept.

---

[164] In fact, the reference is responsible for increasing the dimensionality, but the whole is required to create differentiability along that dimension.

A.3 Higher-Order Logic

Higher-order logic is characterized by the use of references.

Higher-order logic is presented in two sections: first-order logic and abstract logic.

First-order logic is equivalent to a mereological formulation of modern (first-order) symbolic logic. Therefore, the section on first-order logic uses familiar mereological primitives and existential quantification.

Abstract logic is the basis for creating abstract entities. All abstract entities are defined nominally (i.e., in terms of references). Abstract entities are created by the intersection of higher-order entities; that process causes them to be entities of lower dimensionality, therefore they are incapable of being concrete parts. This reduction of dimensionality is also the basis for introducing boundaries and geometric primitives:

- A point is the boundary between two intersecting lines.
- A line is the boundary between two intersecting planes.
- A plane is the boundary between two intersecting solids.

These geometric entities are not explicitly defined here, since their development follows from the fact that the intersection of two higher-order entities can produce an entity of lower dimensionality.[165]

---

[165] If this premise about intersection is not accepted, then an abstract entity such as a point must be taken as primitive, which causes abstract entities to remain at an epistemic distance from concrete entities (unless one introduces the notion of a completed infinity). In other words, although there may be a mapping between discrete referential entities and continuous parts of small size, that mapping is only exact if one subscribes to the philosophy of infinitism.

First-Order Logic

First-order logic allows the use of references via symbolization. Therefore, existential quantifiers (such as $\exists$ or $\forall$) are permitted on the right-hand side of definitions.

Equation 3.1: Existence

$$\exists y \triangleq Ryx \wedge \text{true}(x)$$

Existence is a property of references that holds if the referent is true (in the sense described in the previous section).

Equation 3.2: Universality

$$\forall y \triangleq \neg \exists x : Ryx \wedge \text{false}(x)$$

A reference is true for all entities if there is no referent of that reference for which it is false.

Equation 3.3: Atoms

$$\text{atom}(x) \triangleq \neg \exists z : Pzx$$

A thing is an atom if it has no parts.

Equation 3.4: Universes

$$\text{universe}(x) \triangleq \neg \exists z : Wzx$$

A thing is a universe if it has no wholes.

Equation 3.5: Empty Reference

$$\text{emptyRef}(x) \triangleq Rx \wedge (\neg \exists z : Rxz)$$
$$= \varnothing$$

A reference is empty if its referent does not exist.

Empty references are denoted using the null-set operator.

Equation 3.6: Full Reference

$$\text{fullRef}(x) \triangleq \exists z : Rxz \land \text{universe}(z)$$

A reference is full if it is a reference to a universe.

Equation 3.7: Overlap

$$\text{overlap}(x_1, x_2) \triangleq \exists z : Pzx_1 \land Pzx_2$$

Two entities overlap one another if there is some third entity that is a part of both.

Equation 3.8: Underlap

$$\text{underlap}(x_1, x_2) \triangleq \exists z : Wzx_1 \land Wzx_2$$

Two entities underlap one another if there is some third entity that is a whole of both.

Equation 3.9: Complement

$$\text{complement}(x_1, y) \triangleq x_2 :$$
$$Px_2 y$$
$$\forall z : (Pzx_1 \lor Pzx_2) \implies Pzy$$
$$\neg \exists z : Pzx_1 \land Pzx_2$$
$$\neg \exists z : Pzy \land (\text{overlap}(z, x_1) \lor \text{overlap}(z, x_2))$$

The complement of a part (x_1) with respect to a whole (y) is a second part (x_2) such that:

1. x_2 is part of y.
2. All parts of x_1 or x_2 are parts of the whole y.
3. x_1 and x_2 have no parts in common.
4. There is no part of that whole which does not overlap with either x_1 or x_2.

Equation 3.10: Connected

$$\text{connected}(x_1, x_2) \triangleq \text{overlap}(x_1, x_2) \lor \exists\, \text{boundary}(x_1, x_2)$$

Two entities are connected if they overlap or their boundary exists, where existence of that boundary requires only positive dimensionality.

Equation 3.11: Internal Identity

$$\text{ID}_{\text{int}}(x_1, x_2) \triangleq \forall z : Pzx_1 \Leftrightarrow Pzx_2$$

Two things are internally identical if they have the same parts.

Equation 3.12: External Identity

$$\text{ID}_{\text{ext}}(x_1, x_2) \triangleq \forall z : Wzx_1 \Leftrightarrow Wzx_2$$

Two things are externally identical if they have the same wholes.

Equation 3.13: Mereological Identity

$$\text{ID}_{\text{mer}}(x_1, x_2) \triangleq \text{ID}_{\text{int}}(x_1, x_2) \land \text{ID}_{\text{ext}}(x_1, x_2)$$

Two things are mereologically identical if they are both internally and externally identical.

Equation 3.14: Referential Identity

$$\text{ID}_{\text{ref}}(x, y) \triangleq (x = y) \lor$$
$$\left(\exists z_1, z_2 : Rxz_1 \land Ryz_2 \land \text{ID}_{\text{ref}}(z_1, z_2) \right)$$

Two references are referentially identical if they are equal, or their referents are referentially identical.

Equation 3.15: Nominal Identity

$$\text{ID}_{\text{nom}}(x, y) \triangleq$$
$$\left(\exists z, x_1, y_1 : (Wzx_1 \wedge Rx_1x) \wedge (Wzy_1 \wedge Ry_1y)\right) \vee$$
$$\left(\exists z_1, z_2 : Rz_1x \wedge Rz_2y \wedge \text{ID}_{\text{nom}}(z_1, z_2)\right)$$

Two things are nominally identical if there is a whole that contains references to both, or there are references to each that are nominally identical.

Abstract Logic

Abstract logic describes abstract entities, which are the low-dimensional result of the intersection of higher-order entities.

Equation 3.16: Boundary

$$\text{boundary}(x_1, x_2) \triangleq b :$$
$$b = x_1 \cap x_2$$
$$\dim(b) \geq 0$$
$$\dim(b) + 1 = \dim(x_1) = \dim(x_2)$$

A boundary between two entities (x_1, x_2) is an entity (b) such that:

1. b is the intersection of x_1 and x_2.
2. The dimensionality of b is a non-negative number
3. The dimensionality of b is one less than the dimensionality of x_1 or x_2.

Less formally, a boundary is an intersection of two entities that overlap in some dimensions but not in others. As a result, boundaries are abstract objects, since their dimensionality is less than the dimensionality of the objects that they divide. Hence, the existence of boundaries *as abstract objects* does not require them to have the dimensionality of the containing space.

Appendix B

Reference Material

The symbols and conventions used in this book.

B.1 Symbolic Conventions

An assortment of profound squiggles.

Table B.1a: Epistemic Spaces

Symbol	Epistemic Space
U	Physical space
O	Objective space
S	Subjective space
N	Sensory space
C	Conceptual space
V	Symbolic space

Table B.1b: Epistemic Relations

Symbol	Epistemic Relations
Θ	Sensation
Δ	Action
Φ, φ	Conceptualization, a concept
Ψ, ψ	Visualization, a sensation
Ξ, ξ	Symbolization, a symbol
Ω	Interpretation

Table B.1c: *A priori* Symbols

Operator	Logical Result	Interpretation
$x = \Phi(y, ...)$	Pxy , part(x,y)	x is a part of y
$y = \Psi(x, ...)$	Wyx , whole(y,x)	y is a whole of x
$x = \Xi(y)$	Rxy , reference(x,y)	x is a reference to y
$y = \Omega(x)$	Tyx , referent(y,x)	y is the referent of x

Table B.1d: Logical Symbols

Logical Symbol	Interpretation
=	Equality
$\triangleq$	Definition
$\wedge$	Conjunction (logical and)
$\vee$	Disjunction (logical or)
$\neg$	Negation (logical not) or complement
$\exists$	There exists
$\forall$	For all
$\cup$	Union
$\cap$	Intersection
O	Everything
$\varnothing$	Empty reference (nothing)

B.2 Typographical Conventions

Conventions relating to the way things are written.

In a conversation about a rock, it is sometimes unclear if the thing to which is referred is a physical thing (the rock object), a sensory thing (the rock sensation), a conceptual thing (the rock concept), or a symbolic thing (the name for the rock concept). To disambiguate between these different uses, the following conventions are adopted:

- "Rock" without typographic augmentation generally refers to the rock object.
- "Rock$_\psi$" refers to the sensation of the rock.
- "Rock$_\varphi$" refers to the concept of the rock.
- "Rock$_\xi$" refers to the symbol of the rock.

These particular lower-case greek letters are used because they are the result of visualization (Ψ), conceptualization (Φ), and symbolization (Ξ) operations. In particular, Rock$_\psi$ = Ψ(Rock$_\varphi$), Rock$_\varphi$ = Φ(Rock$_\psi$), and Rock$_\xi$ = Ξ(Rock$_\varphi$).

Further, the concept of a rock may exist as a zeroth-order concept or a higher-order concept. To indicate the order of a concept, a superscript may be used:

- "Rock^0" indicates a zeroth-order concept.
- "Rock^n" indicates an nth-order concept (where n is some positive integer).
- "Rock$^+$" indicates a higher-order concept (i.e., order 1 or more).

Finally, there are several other typographic conventions which have somewhat specific connotations in this work:

- Forward slashes are used to indicate dichotomies, as in subjective/objective.

- Hyphens are used for making compound-words.

- Emphasis is denoted *like this*, as are titles, foreign words, and mathematical variables.

- Glossary entries and intra-document references are underlined, and are hyperlinks in electronic versions of the book: <u>self-reference</u>.

- Bibliographic references and URLs are enclosed in square brackets to avoid syntactic ambiguity, as in [<u>http:// theWholePart.com</u>].

- The car having the wheel as a part is equivalent to the wheel having the car as a whole.

- Parentheses are allowed to nest (sometimes (if one is careful to close them)).

- This work uses *logical punctuation*. For example, punctuation is placed within quotes only if it belongs to the "quoted material".

- The affirming negation of an object x is written as not-x, and the non-affirming negation of that object is written as non-x.

B.3 Ideographic Conventions

Conventions relating to diagrams.

The diagrams used in this work follow a syntax which is loosely based on UML (the Unified Modeling Language). UML depicts things and relations as shapes and arrows. Things of various kinds are represented with ellipses, as in Figure B.3a.

Figure B.3a: Things are represented as ellipses.

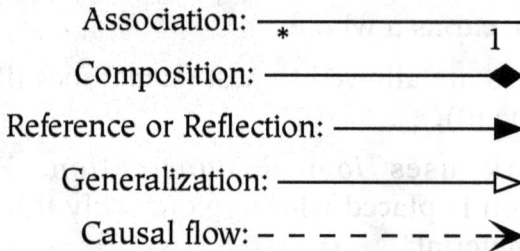

Figure B.3b: Relations of various kinds are depicted using lines with various arrowheads.

The relations between things are depicted using the different types of arrows shown in Figure B.3b. Relations with a solid line are structural, while those relations with a dashed line indicate transformation or movement.

◆ **Association:** Association depicts an arbitrary relation between two entities. Since association has no arrowhead, it is a bidirectional relation. The labels on the association line above indicate that it is many-to-one, or that many of the things on the left are associated with one of the things on the right.[166]

- **Composition**: The composition arrow points from a part to its whole.

- **Reference**: The reference arrow points from a reference to its referent.

- **Generalization**: The generalization arrow points from a subtype to its supertype (i.e., the thing on the left is a type of the thing on the right).

- **Causal Flow**: Causal flow shows general movement. The relations of the basic model of cognition are all variations of this arrow.

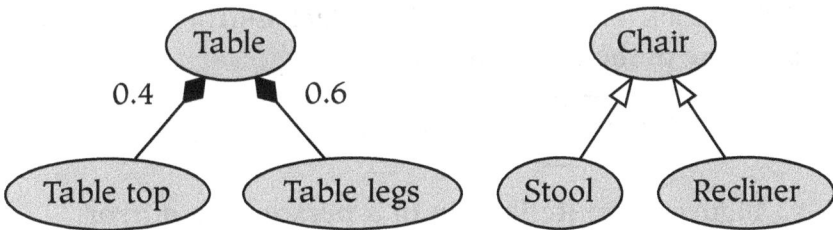

Figure B.3c: Example part and type hierarchies.

Things and relations are used to create hierarchies, as shown in Figure B.3c. The relative left-right position of the children is not meaningful, since no structural element has been drawn between them to establish a relation. That said, it is common to draw hierarchies with the largest or most general node at the top and proceed downwards. The labels on the meronomy at left (0.4 and 0.6) indicate the volume of each part relative to the whole. Since the volume of the table top and table legs add up to 1.0, there are no other parts of the table besides the top and the legs (assuming that the top and the legs do not overlap).

The introduction of labels to indicate the degree of parthood can also be used to depict overlap. As overlap is not defined in UML, it can be visually depicted as bidirectional composition,

---

[166] "*" is called the Kleene star, and indicates a multiplicity.

where the diamond arrowheads corresponding to composition are annotated with the degree to which they are a part. For example, Figure B.3d shows overlap between two parts, where 30% of part$_1$ overlaps with 40% of part$_2$.

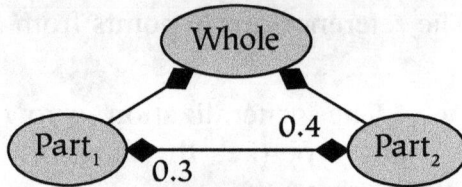

Figure B.3d: Overlap of two parts.

References or reflections can also be depicted as bidirectional, as in Figure B.3e, which illustrates that just as mirrors reflect people that look at them, people reflect mirrors at which they look (in virtue of their mental references).

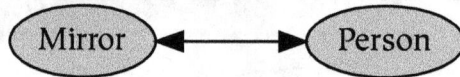

Figure B.3e: Reflection of a person in a mirror, and a mirror in a person.

Glossary

absolute: A thing is absolute if it does not depend on other things and relative if it does depend on other things. Conceptually, the parts of a thing form its absolute nature, and the wholes of a thing form its relative nature.

abstract: Concepts are abstract if their dimensionality is lower than a concrete concept. The degree of abstraction is therefore related to its <u>conceptual order</u>: zeroth-order concepts are concrete and higher-order concepts are abstract.

atom: An atom is an indivisible thing.

awareness: In the context of this book, awareness is intentional; awareness is always awareness of something *else*. The term <u>consciousness</u> is used when a more general meaning is intended.

basic categories: Basic categories are "... 'in the middle' of a general-to-specific hierarchy. Generalization proceeds 'upward' from the basic level and specialization proceeds 'downward'." [<u>Lakoff, 2008</u>]. Experimentally, basic categories are basic in the sense that they are known better, as measured by cue validity.

boundary: Boundaries are nominal objects that have an extent of zero along the dimension which they divide. Therefore, boundaries create parts that are *connected*. For a more substantial discussion, see [Varzi, 2015].

chunking: Chunking is the cognitive process by which multiple concepts in short-term memory are turned into a single concept. It is roughly synonymous with unitization.

complement: The complement of a part is defined as the whole of that part, less that part.

concept: A concept is a part of the conceptual universe. It serves as the basis of thought, it is a whole of sensations, other concepts, or symbols, and can in turn be referenced by a symbol.

conceptual order: Conceptual order indicates the number of symbols that must be traversed in order to reach ontological ground. Zeroth-order concepts consist of sensation and other zeroth-order concepts, while higher-order concepts consist of symbols (or references to constituent concepts). It is also possible for concepts to be composed of other concepts directly (as unitizations), in which case they have a higher epistemic level but not a higher order.

concrete: See abstract.

consciousness: In the context of this book, consciousness is understood as *phenomenal consciousness*, rather than *access consciousness* (see [Block, 1995]). Consciousness may be reflexive or intransitive, in which case it is not mediated by references. See also awareness.

contiguous: A thing is (spatially) contiguous if its parts are connected, or discontiguous if its parts are not connected.

deep structure: The deep structure of a sentence, as opposed to its surface structure, is the underlying syntactic structure that determines how its semantic value can be computed from its various syntactic parts (i.e., the words).

dichotomy: A dichotomy is an operation that divides a whole into two parts.

dimension: A dimension is an axis that allows discrimination along its length. It may be nominal, ordinal, interval, or ratio.

direct realism: Direct realism entails that the mind directly engages with external reality. Indirect realism entails that the mind consists of representations of an external reality, and that there is consciousness only of these representations (i.e., and not of external reality itself). Indirect realism is also known as representationalism, or the Representational Theory of Mind (RTM). It is often contrasted with views such as the Computational Theory of Mind (CTM), which posit that mind is a result of mental operations. For a modern treatment, see [Fodor, 2008], [Lycan, 2019], or [Pitt, 2018].

discontiguous: See contiguous.

Dual Process Theory: The theory that the mind can be roughly divided into two systems or processes, one intuitive (System 1) and one rational (System 2). In the Dual Process context, intuitive thinking is called Type 1 and symbolic thinking is called Type 2.

epistemic level: The epistemic level (or referential level) of an entity is its distance from some ontological ground, which has an epistemic level of zero. See also conceptual order and section *Recursion* (p. 88).

epistemological priority: An entity is epistemologically prior to another if it has a lower epistemic level.

epistemology: Epistemology is the study of knowledge. Ontology is the study of being or existence.

equivalence class: An equivalence class is a set of things whose members are equal or equivalent. Equivalence classes are created by wholes of references. See nominal identity.

existence: Existence is a property exclusively of references. If a reference exists, then it can be validly dereferenced (i.e., its reference has a location).

extension: See intension.

external identity: See <u>internal identity</u>.

feature space: A *feature space* is a space that consist of features. For example, visual space is a 3-D space augmented with the feature of color.

finitism: Mathematically, finitism entails that <u>infinity</u> is a process, while infinitism entails that infinity is a completed process or a number (as required for infinitesimal points or infinite sets). For more details, see the essays section of the companion web site, [http://theWholePart.com/essays].

Flatland: Flatland is a two-dimensional world that was originally described by Edwin Abbott [Abbott & Stewart, 2008]. Three-dimensional people do enter that land, but they have unexplainable and magical properties from the point of view of the people of Flatland.

generalization: Generalization refers to the way that a higher-order concept becomes abstract. For example, a conceptual whole can generalize across its parts by isolating their common features. See also <u>unitization</u>.

hierarchy: A hierarchy is a tree-like structure that consists of one or more dimensions. Two prominent types of taxonomies are *meronomies*, which are hierarchies composed of concrete parts and wholes, and *taxonomies*, which are hierarchies composed of abstract parts and wholes.

holism: Holism explains a system in terms of its wholes. Reductionism explains a system in terms of its parts. Both are biased views in that they presuppose that their own explanation is more valid or fundamental than other alternatives.

idea: The idea corresponding to a given concept is the activation of that concept along with its *mereological context*, or all of its parts and wholes.

indirect realism: See <u>direct realism</u>.

infinity: Infinity is often understood as a number that is bigger than any other number, although it is better understood as a limit process with no upper bound (at least according to <u>finitism</u>).

intension: The intension of a set is a characteristic property of all members of that set. The extension of a set is the enumeration of the elements of that set.

intentionality: Intentionality is a philosophical term that indicates a sense of *aboutness*. For example, awareness is intentional because it is always awareness *of* something else (and therefore inherently dualistic).

internal identity: Internal identity establishes the identity of an object in terms of its parts. External identity establishes the identity of an object in terms of its wholes.

isomorphism: Isomorphism, which literally means "the same shape", is a relation between two things that expresses equivalence or congruence of shape. In referential space, a reference is isomorphic to its referent if they are internally and externally identical within their respective domains.

mereology: Mereology is the study of parts and wholes. As a mathematical science, it was originally developed by the Polish philosopher Stanislaw Lesniewski.

metaconcept: A metaconcept is a particular kind of higher-order concept whose purpose is to equate a word and its object by composing both of their symbols. It is a key component of the proposed mechanism for language: the symbol of the word activates the metaconcept, which causes the subsequent interpretation and visualization of the symbol for the object.

negative entity: A *negative entity* is a concept that cannot possibly be sensed such as a hole in the ground, that is known only in virtue of the lack of sensation of dirt. A *positive entity* is a concept that can only be sensed, and which is known only bottom-up.

nominal identity: Nominal identity entails that two entities are identical in virtue of being designated by the same name or type. For example, me from eight years ago is the same me that woke up today because I have the same name now that I did then.

nominalism: Nominalism is a philosophical doctrine that claims that objects in the world are only nominally identical from moment to moment, and not intrinsically identical (see nominal identity). Nominalism is opposed to philosophical realism, which typically maintains that reality is composed of natural kinds. Believers in natural kinds hold that objects have an essence in virtue of which they remain the same from moment to moment. For example, I am the same person now that I was eight years ago because of certain enduring and essential properties.

object: An object is a physical thing, as opposed to sensations and concepts which are different forms of mental things.

object permanence: Object permanence entails knowing that unobserved objects continue to exist in an external world. This requires that a concept is developed for an object that exists independently of the sensation of that object. Object permanence as a developmental stage was first studied by the psychologist Jean Piaget.

ontology: See epistemology.

open: If a space is *open*, or open from above and open from below, then there are no ultimate mereological limits such as largest universes or smallest atoms. Dimensionality may also be open, such that an open-dimensional space has an unlimited number of dimensions.

orthogonal: Two dimensions are orthogonal if a change in one dimension does not entail a change in the other. In two dimensions, for example, orthogonal lines form a right angle to one another.

overlap: Two objects overlap if they share a common part. Two objects underlap if there is some larger whole that contains both.

panpsychism: Panpsychism is the belief that everything is conscious, or that mind and matter are everywhere coextensive. See [Goff & Seager, 2017].

part: A part is a thing that is contained in another thing, which is called its whole. If the part is strictly smaller than that whole, it is called a *proper* part. Similarly, a thing is a whole if it has parts.

partition: A partition of a thing is a complete and exact decomposition of that thing into some number of parts. Every location within the whole is contained in some part, and no location is contained in more than one part.

particular: A *particular* object is a concrete, individual object, such as a specific horse, which may be seen as a collection of universals. A *universal* is a property such as horseness that may apply to multiple particular horses.

percept: A percept is a combination of a concept and its associated sense data. A percept is a part of perceptual space that exists in a continuum between sensory and conceptual spaces.

positive entity: See negative entity.

prototype theory: Prototype theory is proposal within cognitive psychology that pertains to the understanding of cognitive categories, and which is often contrasted with exemplar theory.

realism: See nominalism.

reductionism: See holism.

reference: A reference is a representation of a thing, as opposed to the thing itself. Linguistically, references may be either lightweight *signs* or heavyweight *symbols*. A reference names or refers to a referent.

referent: See reference.

reflection: Reflection is a continuous version of (discrete) reference.

relative: See absolute.

self-reference: See self-reference.

sensation: A sensation is a part of sensory space. It constitutes nonconceptual mental content and is a subjective referent to

223

either an object or a concept (in the latter case, it is called a symbol).

set of all sets: The set of all sets (or the Universal Set) is that set which is composed of all sets. If not created using constructivist principles, it creates paradoxes such as the Russell-Zermelo Paradox (see [Irvine & Deutsch, 2016]).

space: Space is used in this book as a metaphor for both reality and mind. It operates as a subsymbolic replacement for discrete entities.

subsymbolic: In the context of cognitive science, theories such as connectionism offer a subsymbolic alternative to traditional symbolic approaches. In mathematics, a similar distinction exists between point-free topologies such as mereology and point-set topology. See also subsymbol.

symbol: A symbol is a sensation that references a concept. The term "symbol" as used in this book entails a cognitive symbol, as opposed to verbal or written symbols that exist independently of mind. See also subsymbolic.

thing: A thing is a generic term that is further differentiated into objects, sensations, concepts, and symbols; for further details, see section *Epistemic Universes* (p. 60).

token: A token is an instance of a type. For example, there are two tokens of the word "a" in the previous sentence, but those tokens consist of a single type. A type is also called a *class* of things.

type: See token.

underlap: See overlap.

unitization: Unitization refers to the process of making wholes as unions of parts. It does not entail generalization.

universal: See particular.

universe: A universe is a space that is an *ultimate whole* from some particular point of reference.

whole: See <u>part</u>.

226

Bibliography

Abbott & Stewart, 2008: Abbott, E. A., & Stewart, I. (2008). *The annotated flatland: A romance of many dimensions*. New York, NY: Basic Books.

Armstrong, 2010: Armstrong, D. M. (2010). *Universals: An opinionated introduction*. Boulder, CO: Westview Press.

Austin, 2005: Austin, J. H. (2005). *Zen and the brain: Toward an understanding of meditation and consciousness*. Cambridge, MA: MIT Press.

Baddeley, 2001: Baddeley, A. (2001). The Concept of Episodic Memory. *Philosophical Transactions: Biological Sciences, 356*(1413), 1345–1350.

Baylor & Lamb, 1979: Baylor, D. A., Lamb, T., & Yau, K.-W. (1979). Responses of retinal rods to single photons. *The Journal of Physiology, 288*(1), 613–634.

Bermudez & Cahen, 2015: Bermúdez, J., & Cahen, A. (2015). Nonconceptual mental content. In E. N. Zalta (Ed.), *The Stanford Encyclopedia of Philosophy* (Fall 2015). Metaphysics Research Lab, Stanford University. [https://plato.stanford.edu/archives/fall2015/entries/content-nonconceptual/]

Bernays, 1991: Bernays, P. (1991). *Axiomatic set theory*. New York, NY: Dover Publications.

Block, 1983: Block, N. (Ed.). (1983). *Readings in philosophy of psychology*. Vol. 1. Cambridge, MA: Harvard University Press.

Block, 1995: Block, N. (1995). On a confusion about a function of consciousness. *Behavioral and Brain Sciences, 18*(2), 227–247.

Bohm, 2002: Bohm, D. (2002). *Wholeness and the implicate order*. New York, NY: Routledge.

Boole, 2003: Boole, G. (2003). *The laws of thought*. Amherst, NY: Prometheus Books.

Braitenberg, 2004: Braitenberg, V. (2004). *Vehicles: Experiments in synthetic psychology*. Cambridge, MA: MIT Press.

Capra, 1992: Capra, F. (1992). *The Tao of physics: An exploration of the parallels between modern physics and Eastern mysticism*. London, United Kingdom: Flamingo.

Casati, 2009: Casati, R. (2009). Surfaces, holes, shadows. In R. L. Poidevin (Ed.), *The Routledge Companion to Metaphysics*, 382–388. Routledge.

Casati & Varzi, 1999: Casati, R., & Varzi, A. C. (1999). *Parts and places: The structures of spatial representation*. Cambridge, MA: MIT Press.

Chomsky, 1980: Chomsky, N. (1980). *Rules and representations*. New York, NY: Columbia University Press.

Chomsky, 1995: Chomsky, N. (1995). *Aspects of the theory of syntax*. Cambridge, MA: MIT Press.

Churchland, 1988: Churchland, P. M. (1988). *Matter and consciousness: A contemporary introduction to the philosophy of mind*. Cambridge, MA: MIT Press.

Dennett, 1991: Dennett, D. C. (1991). *Consciousness explained*. Boston, MA: Little, Brown and Co.

Dogen et al., 2013: Dōgen, Tanahashi, K., & Levitt, P. (2013). *The essential Dogen: Writings of the great zen master*. Boston, MA: Shambhala.

Domjan & Burkhard, 1993: Domjan, M., & Burkhard, B. (1993). *The principles of learning and behavior.* Pacific Grove, CA: Brooks/ Cole Publication Co.

Einstein, 1924: Einstein, A. (1924). *Relativity: The special and the general theory* (R. W. Lawson, Trans.). London, United Kingdom: Methuen & Co Ltd.

Einstein & Sullivan, 1972: Einstein, A., & Sullivan. (1972, March 29). The Einstein papers: a man of many parts. *New York Times,* p1 [https://www.nytimes.com/1972/03/29/archives/the-einstein-papers-a-man-of-many-parts-the-einstein-papers-man-of.html]

Evans & Stanovich, 2013: Evans, J. St. B. T., & Stanovich, K. E. (2013). Dual-process theories of higher cognition: Advancing the Debate. *Perspectives on Psychological Science, 8*(3), 223–241. [https://doi.org/10.1177/1745691612460685]

Fodor, 2008: Fodor, J. A. (2008). *LOT 2: The language of thought revisited.* Oxford, United Kingdom: Oxford University Press.

Gallistel, 1993: Gallistel, C. R. (1993). *The Organization of learning.* Cambridge, MA: MIT Press.

Ganeri, 2012: Ganeri, J. (2012). *The self: Naturalism, consciousness, and the first-person stance.* Oxford, United Kingdom: Oxford University Press.

Gardenfors, 2004: Gärdenfors, P. (2004). *Conceptual spaces: The geometry of thought.* Cambridge, MA: MIT Press.

Gersho & Grey, 2003: Gersho, A., & Gray, R. M. (2003). *Vector quantization and signal compression.* Boston, MA: Kluwer.

Gladwell, 2007: Gladwell, M. (2007). *Blink: The power of thinking without thinking.* New York, NY: Back Bay Books.

Goff & Seager, 2017: Goff, W., Philip, Seager, & Allen-Hermanson, S. (2017). Panpsychism. In E. N. Zalta (Ed.), *The Stanford Encyclopedia of Philosophy (Winter 2017).* [https://plato.stanford.edu/archives/win2017/entries/panpsychism/]

Grossberg, 1988: Grossberg, S. (Ed.). (1988). *Neural networks and natural intelligence*. Cambridge, MA: MIT Press.

Gyamtso, 1988: Gyamtso, T. & Hookham, S. K. (Ed.). (1988). *Progressive Stages of Meditation on Emptiness*. Oxford, United Kingdom: Longchen Foundation.

Hanh, 1998: Thich Nhat Hanh (1998). *Mindful Consumption*. Dharma talk, July 17, 1998. Plum Village, France.

Hansen, 2017-1: Hansen, C. (2017). Zhuangzi. In E. N. Zalta (Ed.), *The Stanford Encyclopedia of Philosophy (Spring 2017)*. [https://plato.stanford.edu/archives/spr2017/entries/zhuangzi/]

Hein, 2010: Hein, J. L. (2010). *Discrete structures, logic, and computability*. Boston, MA: Jones and Bartlett.

Hofstadter & Dennett, 1988: Hofstadter, D. R., & Dennett, D. C. (Eds.). (1988). *The mind's I: Fantasies and reflections on self and soul*. Toronto, Canada: Bantam Books.

Huang et al., 2006: Huang, A. L., Chen, X., Hoon, M. A., Chandrashekar, J., Guo, W., Tränkner, D., Ryba, N. J. P., & Zuker, C. S. (2006). The cells and logic for mammalian sour taste detection. *Nature, 442*(7105), 934–938. [https://doi.org/10.1038/nature05084]

Hyde & Raffman, 2018: Hyde, D., & Raffman, D. (2018). Sorites paradox. In E. N. Zalta (Ed.), *The Stanford Encyclopedia of Philosophy* (Summer 2018). Metaphysics Research Lab, Stanford University. [https://plato.stanford.edu/archives/sum2018/entries/sorites-paradox/]

Ingram & Tallant, 2018: Ingram, D., & Tallant, J. (2018). Presentism. In E. N. Zalta (Ed.), *The Stanford Encyclopedia of Philosophy* (Spring 2018). Metaphysics Research Lab, Stanford University. [https://plato.stanford.edu/archives/spr2018/entries/presentism/]

Irvine & Deutsch, 2016: Irvine, A. D., & Deutsch, H. (2016). Russell's Paradox. In E. N. Zalta (Ed.), *The Stanford Encyclopedia of Philosophy* (Winter 2016). [https://plato.stanford.edu/archives/win2016/entries/russell-paradox/]

Jackendoff, 1994: Jackendoff, R. (1994). *Patterns in the mind: Language and human nature.* New York, NY: BasicBooks.

Jackendoff, 2007: Jackendoff, R. (2007). *Language, consciousness, culture: Essays on mental structure.* Cambridge, MA: MIT Press.

Jackendoff, 2009: Jackendoff, R. (2009). *Foundations of language: Brain, meaning, grammar, evolution.* Oxford, United Kingdom: Oxford University Press.

Jennings, 2015: Jennings, C. (2015). The standard theory of conscious perception. *Proceedings of the 37th Annual Meeting of the Cognitive Science Society.*

Kahneman, 2013: Kahneman, D. (2013). *Thinking, fast and slow.* New York, NY: Farrar, Straus and Giroux.

Kant, 1781: Kant, I., & Meiklejohn, J. M. D. (1990). *Critique of pure reason.* Buffalo, NY: Prometheus Books.

Kellner, 2011: Kellner, B. (2011). *Self-awareness (svasamvedana) and Infinite Regresses: A Comparison of Arguments by Dignāga and Dharmakīrti.* Journal of Indian Philosophy, 39(4/5), 411–426.

Koerth-Baker, 2010: Koerth-Baker, M. (2010, November). *Kids (and animals) who fail classic mirror tests may still have sense of self.* Scientific American.

Lakoff & Núñez, 2011: Lakoff, G., & Núñez, R. E. (2011). *Where mathematics comes from: How the embodied mind brings mathematics into being.* New York, NY: Basic Books.

Lakoff, 2008: Lakoff, G. (2008). *Women, fire, and dangerous things: What categories reveal about the mind.* Chicago, IL: The University of Chicago Press.

Langer, 1967: Langer, S. K. K. (1967). *An introduction to symbolic logic.* New York, NY: Dover Publications.

Levine, 2000: Levine, D. S. (2000). *Introduction to neural and cognitive modeling.* Mahwah, NJ: Lawrence Erlbaum Associates Publishers.

Lewis, 1991: Lewis, D. K. (1991). *Parts of classes*. Oxford, United Kingdom: Blackwell.

Libet, 1985: Libet, B. (1985). Unconscious cerebral initiative and the role of conscious will in voluntary action. *Behavioral and Brain Sciences*, 8(4), 529-539.

Linnebo & Shapiro, 2019: Linnebo, Ø., & Shapiro, S. (2019). Actual and Potential Infinity. *Noûs*, 53(1), 160–191. [https://doi.org/10.1111/nous.12208]

Longchenpa & Barron, 2007: Longchenpa, D. & Barron, R. (2007). *The precious treasury of philosophical systems: A treatise elucidating the meaning of the entire range of spiritual approaches*. Junction City, CA: Padma Publications.

Lycan, 1998: Lycan, W. G. (Ed.). (1998). *Mind and cognition: A reader*. Oxford, United Kingdom: Blackwell.

Lycan, 2019: Lycan, W. (2019). Representational theories of consciousness. In E. N. Zalta (Ed.), *The Stanford Encyclopedia of Philosophy* (Fall 2019). Metaphysics Research Lab, Stanford University. [https://plato.stanford.edu/archives/fall2019/entries/consciousness-representational/]

Lyons, 1981: Lyons, J. (1981). *Language and linguistics: An introduction*. Cambridge, United Kingdom: Cambridge University Press.

Markosian, 2016: Markosian, N. (2016). Time. In E. N. Zalta (Ed.), *The Stanford Encyclopedia of Philosophy* (Fall 2016). Metaphysics Research Lab, Stanford University. [https://plato.stanford.edu/archives/fall2016/entries/time/]

Maturana & Varela, 1992: Maturana, H. R., & Varela, F. J. (1992). *The tree of knowledge: The biological roots of human understanding*. Boston, MA: Shambhala.

Minsky & Lee, 1988: Minsky, M., & Lee, J. (1988). *The society of mind*. New York, NY: Simon & Schuster.

Minsky, 2006: Minsky, M. (2006). *The emotion machine: Commonsense thinking, artificial intelligence, and the future of the human mind.* New York, NY: Simon & Schuster.

Moltmann, 2003: Moltmann, F. (2003). *Parts and wholes in semantics.* Oxford, United Kingdom: Oxford University Press.

Nagel, 1989: Nagel, T. (1989). *The view from nowhere.* New York, NY: Oxford University Press.

Percy, 2000: Percy, W. (2000). *The message in the bottle: How queer man is, how queer language is, and what one has to do with the other.* New York, NY: Picador.

Pinker, 1997: Pinker, S. (1997). *How the mind works.* New York, NY: Norton.

Pinker, 2000: Pinker, S. (2000). *Words and rules: The ingredients of language.* New York, NY: Perennial.

Pinker, 2007: Pinker, S. (2007). *The stuff of thought: Language as a window into human nature.* New York, NY: Viking.

Pitt, 2018: Pitt, D. (2018). Mental representation. In E. N. Zalta (Ed.), *The Stanford Encyclopedia of Philosophy* (Winter 2018). Metaphysics Research Lab, Stanford University. [https://plato.stanford.edu/archives/win2018/entries/mental-representation/]

Potter, 2004: Potter, M. D. (2004). *Set theory and its philosophy: A critical introduction.* Oxford, United Kingdom: Oxford University Press.

Quine, 1969: Quine, W. V. (1969). *Ontological relativity and other essays.* New York, NY: Columbia University Press.

Quine, 1980: Quine, W. V. (1980). *From a logical point of view: 9 logico-philosophical essays.* Cambridge, MA: Harvard University Press.

Quine, 2001: Quine, W. V. (2001). *Word and object.* Cambridge, MA: MIT Press.

Reicher, 2019: Reicher, M. (2019). Nonexistent objects. In E. N. Zalta (Ed.), *The Stanford Encyclopedia of Philosophy (Winter 2019)*. Retrieved from [https://plato.stanford.edu/archives/win2019/entries/nonexistent-objects/]

Rogers, 1995: Alec Rogers. (2005, June 1). *Temporal and spatial variability in animal cognition*. Retrieved from [http://theWholePart/essays/thesis]

Rucker, 1983: Rucker, R. v. B. (1983). *Infinity and the mind: The science and philosophy of the infinite*. Canada: Bantam Books.

Russel, 1972: Russell, B. (1972). *A history of western philosophy*. New York, NY: Simon and Schuster.

Sacks, 1985: Sacks, O. (1985). *The man who mistook his wife for a hat and other clinical tales*. New York, NY: Summit Books.

Scarantino & de Sousa, 2018: Scarantino, A., & de Sousa, R. (2018). Emotion. In E. N. Zalta (Ed.), *The Stanford Encyclopedia of Philosophy (Winter 2018)*. [https://plato.stanford.edu/archives/win2018/entries/emotion/]

Schwartz & Reisberg, 1991: Schwartz, B., & Reisberg, D. (1991). *Learning and memory*. New York, NY: Norton.

Shantideva & Wallace, 1997: Shantideva, Wallace, V. A., & Wallace, B. A. (1997). *A guide to the Bodhisattva way of life: Bodhicharyavatara*. Ithaca, NY: Snow Lion Publications.

Simons, 2000: Simons, P. M. (2000). *Parts: A study in ontology*. New York, NY: Oxford University Press.

Sorensen, 2019: Sorensen, R. (2019). Nothingness. In E. N. Zalta (Ed.), *The Stanford Encyclopedia of Philosophy (Summer 2019)*. [https://plato.stanford.edu/archives/sum2019/entries/nothingness/]

Stjernfelt, 2007: Stjernfelt, F. (2007). *Diagrammatology: An investigation on the borderlines of phenomenology, ontology, and semiotics*. Dordrecht, Netherlands: Springer.

Thakchoe, 2011: Thakchoe, S. (2017). The theory of two truths in India. In E. N. Zalta (Ed.), *The Stanford Encyclopedia of*

Philosophy (Spring 2017). Metaphysics Research Lab, Stanford University. [https://plato.stanford.edu/archives/spr2017/entries/twotruths-india/]

Thanissaro, 2013: Thanissaro Bhikkhu. (2013). Satipatthana sutta: frames of reference (Thanissaro Bhikkhu, Trans.). *Access to Insight (BCBS Edition)*, Majjhima Nikaya 10. [http://www.accesstoinsight.org/tipitaka/mn/mn.010.than.html]

Tiles, 2004: Tiles, M. (2004). *The philosophy of set theory: An historical introduction to Cantor's paradise.* Mineola, NY: Dover Publications.

Varela, Thompson & Rosch, 2000: Varela, F. J., Thompson, E., & Rosch, E. (2000). *The embodied mind: Cognitive science and human experience.* Cambridge, MA: MIT Press.

Varzi, 2015: Varzi, A. (2015). Boundary. In E. N. Zalta (Ed.), *The Stanford Encyclopedia of Philosophy* (Winter 2015). Metaphysics Research Lab, Stanford University. [https://plato.stanford.edu/archives/win2015/entries/boundary/]

Wasserman, 2018: Wasserman, R. (2018). Material constitution. In E. N. Zalta (Ed.), *The Stanford Encyclopedia of Philosophy* (Fall 2018). Metaphysics Research Lab, Stanford University. [https://plato.stanford.edu/archives/fall2018/entries/material-constitution/]

Wilson et al., 1989: Wilson, T. D., Dunn, D. S., Kraft, D., & Lisle, D. J. (1989). Introspection, attitude change, and attitude-behavior consistency: The disruptive effects of explaining why we feel the way we do. In *Advances in experimental social psychology 22*, 287–343. Elsevier.

Zahavi, 2008: Zahavi, D. (2008). *Subjectivity and selfhood: Investigating the first-person perspective.* Cambridge, MA: MIT Press.

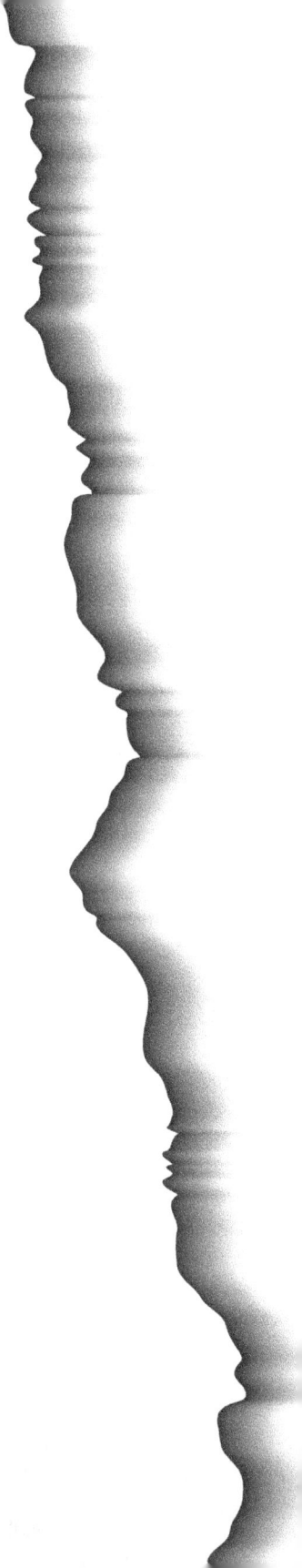

www.ingramcontent.com/pod-product-compliance
Lightning Source LLC
Chambersburg PA
CBHW060448280326
41933CB00014B/2698